GOING, GOING, GONE!

GOING, GOING, GONE!

The Art of the Trade in Major League Baseball

Fran Zimniuch

TAYLOR TRADE PUBLISHING
Lanham • New York • Boulder • Toronto • Plymouth, UK

Published by Taylor Trade Publishing
An imprint of The Rowman & Littlefield Publishing Group, Inc.
4501 Forbes Boulevard, Suite 200, Lanham, Maryland 20706
www.rlpgtrade.com

Estover Road, Plymouth PL6 7PY, United Kingdom

Distributed by NATIONAL BOOK NETWORK

Library of Congress Cataloging-in-Publication Data

Zimniuch, Fran.
  Going, going, gone! : the art of the trade in major league baseball / Fran Zimniuch.
    p. cm.
  Includes bibliographical references and index.
  ISBN-13: 978-1-58979-334-7 (pbk. : alk. paper)
  ISBN-10: 1-58979-334-X (pbk. : alk. paper)
  1. Baseball players—Trading of—United States—History. I. Title.

GV880.3.Z55 2008
796.357'64—dc22

2007039237

⊗ ™ The paper used in this publication meets the minimum requirements of American National Standard for Information Sciences—Permanence of Paper for Printed Library Materials, ANSI/NISO Z39.48-1992.

Manufactured in the United States of America.

*This is for the baseball lifers
mentioned in these pages who have made
baseball so enjoyable over the years and who have
occasionally knocked our socks off with a true
blockbuster trade.
It is also for those in my life who have
knocked my socks off,
including my sons, Brent and Kyle.*

CONTENTS

FOREWORD

As a former general manager of the Los Angeles Dodgers, I know full well what goes into the making of a baseball trade. I experienced both high points and low points when it came to the results of trades during my twelve seasons as the GM of the Dodgers.

General managers often are judged solely on the trades they have made. Fair or unfair, that usually is the way it plays out in the public forum.

Whereas a general manager sees the trading of players as a way of improving his team, the fan seizes upon the news of a trade to play the role of GM. The fan also has the advantage of waiting until some or all of the results play out before fully declaring his opinion of a deal. There is no such luxury for the general manager.

Few transactions in the history of Major League Baseball have gained the attention that is caused by a trade—not the signing of a free agent player and certainly not the selection of a player in baseball's first-year player draft.

There are trades general managers and teams would like to forget, but that is not possible with all of the public scrutiny and the memories of deals that seem to be passed down from one generation of fans to another.

Baseball trades have changed dramatically through the years as free agency has become a major part of the game and salaries have risen at an amazing rate. Furthermore, guaranteed contracts with provisions covering everything one can imagine—including no-trade clauses—have complicated the life of the general manager attempting to make a deal.

Even so, trades are made today just as they have been through the history of baseball, and the results of a deal quite often determine the fate of a pennant race as well as the short-term (sometimes longer) future of an organization.

In this book, Fran Zimniuch examines the history of baseball trades and the changes that have taken place through the years that have impacted trades. Fran has sought out a number of people who have sat in the GM chairs to bring the fans a look at what has taken place behind the scenes.

He also has taken a studious approach to examine some of the major issues in the game, including the reserve clause (chapters 4, 5, and 6) and the negotiations between owners and the players' union.

As always, it is the deals themselves and not the details of a labor negotiation that capture the greatest interest of the baseball fan. Fran reviews historic deals through the years and provides the fans with a look at what was behind the decisions.

One of the deals that caught my personal attention is outlined in chapter 3 ("Hank Sauer and Frankie Baumholtz for Peanuts and The Hat"). The deal was made in 1949; I was a young boy growing up in Jamestown, Ohio, at the time and a fan of the Cincinnati Reds.

My father had left a copy of the *Cincinnati Enquirer* by my bedside and I awoke to find that two of my favorite players on the Reds—Sauer and Baumholtz—had been traded to the Chicago Cubs for Harry "Peanuts" Lowrey and Harry "The Hat" Walker.

How could the Reds make that trade? I asked myself.

I remember that I was very upset and as time went on I had every right to be upset, as Sauer proved to be a top slugger for the

Cubs. It has been nearly six decades and I can still see the headline announcing the deal and recall my reaction.

I know there's a deal or two from my time as the general manager of the Dodgers that fans will remember and that I would like to forget (Pedro Martinez, for one).

The fact is, trades stay with the fans and that adds to the interest in the game.

Pull up a chair, and let Fran Zimniuch help you travel down memory lane, where baseball trades are brought to life.

Fred Claire, former general manager of the Los Angeles Dodgers and author of *Fred Claire: My 30 Years in Dodger Blue*

PREFACE

If you're a real baseball fan, you have to love trades. After all, we fans know better than the baseball lifers like general managers, who do this for a living and for some unknown reason can't make the deals that we all know they should and can make. There is no good reason why they can't make the trades that can turn our favorite nine into a contender. C'mon, how hard can it be? We'll give you Bobby Wine, you give us Willie Mays. It's as simple as that. Or for this generation, you take Tomas Perez, we get A-Rod.

During the off-season, better known by die-hard fans as the hot-stove league, real trades are often made to improve our favorite teams. They are the only thing that makes the off-season the least bit palatable. But there is an old saying that a little bit of knowledge is a dangerous thing. Well, thanks to cable TV and the countless major league games that we are all lucky enough to be able to see during the course of the season, true fans have the opportunity to see players from both leagues many times a week. Much to the chagrin of those aforementioned baseball lifers, fans are actually now more knowledgeable about the unrealistic trades they'd like to see made. Of course, that wasn't always the case.

When I was growing up as a young kid in the 1960s, I saw my first game with my dad at old, rickety Connie Mack Stadium in Philadelphia when the Fighting Phillies took on the Cincinnati

Reds in a twi-night doubleheader. Remember them? Two games for the price of one! I was totally smitten by the game of baseball. Sitting in the upper deck in left field, I can still feel the hot August night air and the thick smell of cigar smoke. (This was also in the day when you could smoke a stogie at the ballpark.)

Since my first game was in Philadelphia, it's only natural that the experience would include fans getting on the players. In the City of Brotherly Love, even the home players get a ribbing. In fact, there are numerous examples of home players getting it worse than visiting players. Hey, if Santa Claus could be pelted with snowballs and booed at a Philadelphia Eagles game, do baseball players actually think they'll get off the hook without a little home-town abuse? From my first ball game, I can still picture Phillies outfielder Wes Covington, wearing number forty-three, who after a few innings began waving the hometown fans away as they con-stantly chanted with Ballantine beer–flavored breath, "Wes is the best, but he needs a rest." His Cincinnati counterpart, future Hall of Famer Frank Robinson, who wore number twenty, was not treated with the same kid gloves that the Phillies faithful laid on Covington. A doubleheader full of beer surely made the players never, ever want to hear the beer jingle, "Hey friend, do it again. Ballantine, Ballantine beer."

My dad talked of seeing more games the following season, but those plans were never to be—he died that winter, before we could continue my baseball education. That doubleheader against the Reds with my dad is one of my fondest memories of him. Although he was gone before my tenth birthday, he helped plant the baseball seed in me, guaranteeing that I would be the type of baseball fan who has four seasons in his life: spring training, the regular season, the postseason, and that damn off-season. Con-cepts such as spring, summer, fall, and winter are incidental ideas that are enjoyed by other people.

It wasn't long before I was learning more and more about the game of baseball, thanks in large part to Hall of Fame outfielder

Richie Ashburn, who became my baseball tutor. He taught me countless truths, strategies, and folklore about the game as he served as a Phillies announcer for more than three decades, giving me a feel for the game that made it enjoyable on many different levels. Even though my dad was gone, just hearing Whitey's voice day after day, game after game, year after year, made the connection even stronger. Baseball was in my blood.

Part of the fun and enjoyment that many of us find in the game also includes discussions and debates about trade rumors that we're all more than willing to share an opinion about. Ever since that innocent time during my childhood when player transactions were made to either improve the club or get rid of a troublemaker who was a cancer on the team, I was hooked not only on the game itself, but on the idea of taking on the fantasy job of handling player transactions. One of the most enjoyable parts of writing books about my one true passion in life is that I've been able to meet and discuss our game with players, owners, general managers, scouts, and other people who actually shape the game I love so dearly. Writing this book was a way to feed my insatiable hunger for a better knowledge and understanding of all aspects of the game. Maybe they could actually make me understand why they couldn't make trades with more ease. After all, how hard can it be?

This book came from my desire to be a sponge and learn as much as I could about our game and share my newfound knowledge with like-minded people. Wouldn't you love to have been a fly on the wall of a smoke-filled room where general managers, scouts, managers, and coaches from two teams went through the process of completing a trade? I sure would have. Or better yet, how about being the bartender at a gin mill where a deal was done, diagrammed on napkins. But as the old Mary Hopkins song lamented, "Those were the days, my friend, we thought they'd never end." But the reality of our game today is that those days have ended and some drastic changes have occurred in baseball, making trading players a much more complicated, seemingly near impossible task. And yet, against all odds, thanks to those afore-mentioned baseball lifers, it happens all the time.

A project such as this one can often take on a life of its own. What began as a much simpler venue to discuss the various types of trades and transactions, while giving some examples of each, has morphed into a historical treatment of the game from its infancy to the present. The focus is on how various influences have changed the way that baseball teams operate, thrive, and make trades in baseball's brave new world.

Arbitration, free agency, no-trade clauses, and other influences have seen scratch pads and bar napkins with player names listed replaced with computer readouts, with tendencies to psychological testing, and with consideration of the various clauses and legalities that fog seemingly every player contract. But at the end of the day, the game is still the same basic game, even with its ugly, red-headed stepchildren, the designated hitter and artificial surfaces.

When I was the child/sponge learning about baseball, the only games that graced the television airwaves were road games of my Phillies and the national Game of the Week, televised every Saturday afternoon, with Curt Gowdy and Tony Kubek doing the announcing. You didn't want to miss the national game because it gave the chance to see lots of players who we rarely got to see perform. In those days, the All-Star Game was an event worth watching on a Saturday afternoon because it was the only chance to see the best players of the game during the summer. And the World Series was something worth running home from school to watch on a weekday afternoon.

Of particular interest to me was when American League games were shown on the Game of the Week. Keep in mind that there was no ESPN, no cable TV, and no pay-per-view. In those days, you saw your home team and its opponents play. That's why I so enjoyed watching the Junior Circuit play where it was possible to finally see the likes of Mickey Mantle, Yogi Berra, Harmon Kille-brew, Zoilo Versalles, Rod Carew, Ken McBride, Dean Chance,

Jim Lonborg, Tony Conigliaro, and a plethora of other mysterious names in baseball box scores who suddenly came to life on the television screen.

Another big difference in the game in those days was that players and their teams became synonymous. You knew that the Minnesota Twins would have Killebrew, Bob Allison, Earl Battey, and big Don Mincher in the lineup. The Dodgers infield would be Wes Parker, Jim Lefebvre, Maury Wills, and Junior Gilliam. The reserve clause was the law of the game and players were bound to the team with which they originally signed into perpetuity. It was a simpler time, when baseball was played by the players and followed by the fans for the pure love of the game. For true fans such as myself, while the pendulum of power has completely swung to the players' side, and while the almighty dollar has in so many ways bastardized the game, there are still three outs per half inning. Even though managers and coaches insist on driving me absolutely nuts by wearing their designer watches during a game that has no time limit, the game itself is still not complete until the final out of the final inning. It doesn't matter what time it is. So let's outlaw the wearing of timepieces on the field, during the game, by managers and coaches!

For all of the changes and differences in the game of our childhood, the leisurely pace of baseball and the gut-wrenching moments when entire seasons ride on a single pitch remain. It's just that the players may very well be participating in those moments the following season with different clubs. Baseball players have become so transient that they could almost resemble millionaire hobos in bus terminals. Oh Randy Johnson, we hardly knew ye!

Even with all of the changes in the game, thankfully, baseball people are still baseball people. And this idea for a book could never have become reality without them. I spoke with numerous baseball lifers who remember the good old days when trades were much easier to consummate, but have transitioned to the brave new world of today with computerized reports, emails, cell phones, long-term contracts, no-trade contracts, text messages, partial-trade clauses, and the specter of losing free-agents-to-be at the end of their current contract. They spoke with honesty and an incredible wealth of knowledge of the nuances of the game that would be best understood by those with graduate degrees from the best universities in the land. A mere thank you seems as feeble as a Texas League single, but thank you anyway.

In addition to countless baseball executives, a special word of thanks goes to numerous former players, baseball historians, and authors who write about the game who also took the time to participate. To a person, they helped me gain a better understanding and deeper perspective that added credibility and realism to the book.

Former players gave their take on how the game has changed, for the better and for the worse. They spoke of numerous topics, including the uprooting of their lives that trades represent and the enormous salaries that today's players enjoy. Sadly, many of the well-paid players of today have no knowledge of and even less interest in the history of the game that made such a living possible. Names such as Curt Flood, Andy Messersmith, Dave McNally, Marvin Miller, and Peter Seitz should be the topic of every Thanksgiving Day toast that today's players give. A special thank you to these former players who spoke of the changes in their game with a love of the game that is still so apparent is in order.

When the idea of this book was in its infancy, my good friend John Warren, a zealot of a baseball fan in the truest sense, sat with me at my beach retreat in Ocean City, New Jersey, one warm summer evening in 2006. We spoke about this idea and my vision for this book. With his genuine smile of approval and positive comments I knew that I was on to something, because if someone like John Warren thought that this idea had merit, a publisher was sure to follow. Thank you, John. I guess you've earned a free copy of yet another one of my books!

Speaking of a publisher, I'd like to express my gratitude to Rick Rinehart and the entire team at Rowman & Littlefield's Taylor Trade Publishing division, who gave me the green light for this project. Much like the first book we collaborated on, *Shortened Seasons*, the experience was fantastic. They were supportive, showed excitement over the concept, and last but certainly not least, understood the reality that a deadline is often like a speed limit on the highway—a good starting point. As anyone who has ever worked on a deadline knows, all the good intentions in the world are not always enough to get a project done, or a book written on time. Life can sometimes get in the way, as it did for me while working on this project. I can't thank Rick and his staff enough for being so understanding and flexible.

My friend Lou Chimenti, an award-winning journalist and baseball fan, helped me with the editing and organization of the plethora of facts and ideas dealing with the history of the game that has led us to this point in baseball. Another award-winning journalist and friend, Christina Mitchell, also lent her much-needed and appreciated editorial guidance to this project. Not to mention some common sense.

My hope is that you will find this book an interesting and entertaining way to increase your knowledge and understanding of the game of baseball. For in baseball, as in life, we can never stop learning. What I learned from the research for this book brought home just how little I knew. I hope that the research, interviews, and information included will make your enjoyment and understanding of our game even stronger.

And I especially hope this book will help you never lose another baseball trivia contest.

INTRODUCTION

Blockbusters, Trades, Waiver Wires, and Fire Sales

"**I**'ll trade you two Hank Aarons for a Willie Mays, a Sandy Koufax, and the Giants team card." As the two young baseball fans sat on the steps in front of the house and made their first attempt at wheeling and dealing, they were no doubt similar to countless other young baseball fans of the 1960s. Of course, they weren't really trading players, they were dealing in baseball cards, the kind that were sold five to a package, which also included a stale piece of pink bubble gum along with the cards. One side of the card showed an "action" picture of the player, while his career statistics and some personal information normally appeared on the flip side.

"No way," the object of the transaction would say. "I ain't trading you my Giants team card. I'll take two Hank Aarons and a Harmon Killebrew, for one Willie Mays and one Koufax. Take it or leave it."

"Deal," the first child would say. The only thing left to completing the "trade" and making the deal official was their own secret general manager's handshake.

No matter what generation of baseball you might belong to, nearly every fan of the game has traded baseball cards, figures, or some other type of baseball memorabilia at some point in time. Of course it was a different world in the 1960s and baseball was quite different as well. In today's brave new world of baseball, the game has changed thanks to astronomical salaries, arbitration, free agency, no-trade clauses, and a new breed of athlete who may be less enamored with the game itself and more interested in the fruits of his labor. The two young baseball fans who swapped baseball cards on the front step in a past generation have to a large degree been replaced by youngsters and older fans alike who now get their baseball fix in fantasy leagues that enable you to form your own teams through drafts, trades, and other types of acquisitions.

While these leagues are mostly available through the internet, even the most high-tech baseball fan has no doubt collected and traded cards as well. It's a pretty safe bet that not only fans with their baseball roots in the 1960s long for the days when baseball cards were swapped back and forth. It's probably an even safer bet-the-house gamble that today's owners and general managers also wish that they could turn back the hands of time, no doubt longing for that secret general manager's handshake. As being a fan of the game has become a much more high-tech experience, trying to operate from within the friendly confines of front office executives has also become completely different in the new millennium.

Early in the history of America's Game, it might well have been almost as easy to make player transactions as it was to exchange baseball cards. Of course, that was before the end of the reserve clause and the aforementioned advent of arbitration, free agency, gargantuan salaries, and no-trade contracts. For that matter, it seems as if the old smoke-filled bar where general managers would bandy about names much like kids did have now been replaced by computers, profit and loss statements, emails, lawyers, and of course, player agents.

Just how do organizations send players from one team to

another? There are numerous ways to make player transactions. Players can be sold from one team to another, released, and signed as free agents. Historically, trades are probably the most well-known and understood way of making transactions. But you can't simply trade a player like an old baseball card. Even in the simplest of circumstances, rules govern each and every transaction.

Certain distinctions need to be made as far as the roster is concerned. There is a 40-man roster that includes the 25-man active roster, plus fifteen additional players who are currently playing in the minor league system of an organization, as well as players who are on the disabled list. The 25-man roster is the active roster of players eligible to play in a given major league game. The other fifteen are not until rosters are expanded in September.

Teams can expand their rosters to up to forty players beginning on September 1 until the end of the regular season, making all forty available to play in the major leagues should they choose. Rarely will a team bring up more than a handful of the fifteen players for the final month of the regular season. But these new additions to the club on September 1, no matter how many, are not eligible to play in the post season.

TRADES: BLOCKBUSTERS AND OTHER TYPES

Any of the players can be traded if they are currently under contract, from the end of the World Series through July, by any major league team. In years gone by, this was a simple exercise that hinged on teams agreeing on which players they'd like to swap. Of course, the aforementioned no-trade and partial no-trade clauses in player contracts in this day and age can cause confusion. Come the dog days of August, trades can be made only after all players involved clear waivers, or are not on the 40-man roster. It doesn't matter if hindsight deems the trade to be a blockbuster or a bust. As has always been the case, the exercise goes on with both teams hoping that the trade with help each club.

Waiver Wires

Any player can be placed on waivers, regardless of the talent level of the player, giving other teams the opportunity to claim him. But even though a team can claim a player off waivers, the original team can still keep the player in question. Should numerous clubs choose to claim a particular player from waivers, the team with the worst record in the player's league gets the first opportunity to make a claim. If the player is not claimed from waivers in three business days, the player has cleared waivers and may be traded, sent to the minors, or simply released. Or, no move with that player might occur. After August 1, only players who have cleared waivers can be dealt to another club.

Waivers can be a real cat-and-mouse game between clubs. All-Stars as well as pedestrian utility players are often waived during the course of a season as a way of gauging what other teams might have an interest in acquiring them. What makes this game particularly interesting is that this waiver wire is a secret within Major League Baseball. No information of waivers is released until a transaction happens. So at various times during the season, future Hall of Famers could be placed on waivers and no one will ever know if they are simply brought back. It's an exercise that gives baseball clubs the flexibility to move players and the knowledge of which of their players are on other clubs' wish lists. It you place your All-Star-caliber third baseman on the waiver wire, you have a potential trading partner in the team that claims the player.

So when a player is claimed off waivers, the original club can rescind the claim and keep the player. They could also arrange a trade with the new team, or simply do nothing and allow the claiming team to assume the player's contract at the expense of a waiver fee.

Quite often as pennant races heat up, teams that believe they have a shot at postseason action will become buyers and arrange deals that they feel will solidify their playoff run at the expense of teams who attempt to build for the future. But there is a serious time constraint, as players acquired after August 31 can play for the remainder of the regular season but are ineligible for the post-season roster. So you can acquire a player for the September pennant drive knowing full well that should you make the postseason tournament, your new player will not be able to play. The only exception to that rule is if a player acquired after August 31 replaces an injured player in the playoffs.

Players to Be Named Later

The rules that separate professional baseball GMs and hot-stove enthusiasts don't end with waiver wires and the 10/5 rule. During one early scene of the movie *Bull Durham*, the protagonist of the film, catcher Crash Davis, introduces himself as the player to be named later. That is another bullet in the chamber that helps management types make trades.

In most cases, when a player is dealt to a team for a player to be named later, that player to be named is usually a minor leaguer. This option can be particularly useful if two teams cannot agree on the player they want, or the player they are willing to lose. These trades must be completed within six months and could include cash instead of a player. As will be elaborated on later in this book, there are examples of players who were actually traded for a player to be named later who was the same player. So in essence, a player could actually be traded for himself. And unlike in the NFL, NHL, and NBA, teams may not trade their draft choices.

Service Time

In what is no doubt an effort to keep just anyone from walking in off the street and becoming a baseball general manager, baseball uses a complicated decimal point system when recording a player's major league service time. In the ultimate version of what frustrated parents used to refer to as "the new math," in calculating a big-league player's service time, the final number is not a true decimal. A full season of service is 172 days. So if a player has 2.160 days of service time, he has played two years and 160 days, just 12 days short of three years of service. There is a good chance that this player could wind up being a Super Two player, who would be eligible for salary arbitration sooner than in three years, the regular wait that the majority of players have. If a player has 150 days of service, his playing time would be recorded at 0.150, just twelve games short of a full season.

Options

If a player is on the 40-man roster, but not on the active major league roster, he is on optional assignment and the organization can freely move him between the major league club and minor league clubs. If a player is on the 40-man roster and not on the 25-man roster for any part of more than three seasons, he is out of options and cannot be assigned to the minor leagues without clearing waivers first. If a major league player is not yet ineligible for free agency and has options remaining, the team can option him to a minor league team. This is normally what happens when a player is sent down to the minor leagues.

Designated for Assignment

When an organization designates a player for assignment, he is removed from the 40-man roster. This allows the team some time to decide what it wants to do with the player and also frees up a roster spot for additional transactions and acquisitions. Once a player is designated for assignment, the team has ten days to trade the player, release the player, or put the player on waivers. If the player clears waivers and no one picks him up, he can be sent outright to the minor leagues. When this happens, he is removed from the 40-man roster and put on a minor league club's roster. The player is still paid the full amount of his major league contract. A player can be outrighted without his consent only one time in his career.

A player with five years of major league service cannot be assigned to a minor league team without his consent, regardless of whether he has already been outrighted once, even if he clears waivers. This is known as Veterans' Consent. If the player refuses to agree to go to the minor leagues, the team then must release him, or keep him on the major league roster. In either case, the player will be paid under the terms of his major league contract. If he is released and signs with a new team, his previous team must pay the difference in salary between the two contracts if the previous one called for a greater salary.

Disabled List

If a medical condition makes it impossible for a player to play, he can be placed on the disabled list. He can be placed on the fifteen-day disabled list, which frees up a spot on the major league active roster so the injured player is replaced for that amount of time. The player cannot play for at least fifteen consecutive days. A player on the fifteen-day disabled list can be moved to the sixty-day disabled list at any time, but the process cannot be reversed. Players can also be placed on either disabled list retroactively for a minimum of ten inactive days and can remain on either list for as long as it takes for them to recover enough to play. Injured players cannot be traded without the consent of the commissioner. They also cannot be optioned to the minor leagues. However, often when a player is coming off the disabled list, he is assigned to a minor league club for a rehabilitation assignment for up to thirty days for pitchers and up to twenty days for position players. This gives the player an opportunity to get back in game condition so that neither he nor his team will suffer when his stay on the disabled list ends and he is placed on the team's active roster.

The Rule 5 Draft

The Rule 5 draft prevents a club from keeping a player with major league potential in the minor leagues while another team would be willing to use him on the major league level. This draft brings home just how important minor league scouts are to an organization, as they often recommend young players who might be ready to compete on the major league level. Two prime examples of outstanding players acquired in this manner are Hall of Famer Roberto Clemente, by Pittsburgh from Brooklyn, and George Bell, by Toronto from Philadelphia.

A player is eligible for the Rule 5 draft in the off-season if he is not on a 40-man roster and has spent three years with a minor league contract first signed when he was nineteen or older. Teams are not forced to pick a player in the Rule 5 draft. But if they choose to do so, the catch is that the chosen player must be kept on the selecting team's 25-man big-league roster for the entire season after the draft, or must be offered back to the team he was on originally. He cannot be optioned or designated to the minor leagues for the upcoming season. So if you pick a young player from Double A ball, he must play the entire season on the big-league level.

He must also be active for at least ninety days, which keeps clubs from hiding a young, green prospect on the disabled list with a mystery injury. Should the Rule 5 draft choice be traded, the new team must keep him on the active roster as well, or offer him back to his original team.

Too complicated? Not worth the trouble? Baseball history is chock-full of great examples of clubs using the Rule 5 draft to strengthen their team. There have been countless outstanding major league players who got their baptism in the major leagues thanks to the Rule 5 draft. All they needed was the opportunity to perform and show their skills.

The list includes players such as Johan Santana, Dan Uggla, Jay

Gibbons, Scott Podsednik, Frank Catalanotto, Willy Taveras, Miguel Batista, Antonio Alfonseca, Luis Ayala, Guillermo Mota, Scott Sauerbeck, Jorge Sosa, Derrick Turnbow, and Shane Victorino. So the payoff can be well worth the effort and once again brings home the importance of having quality scouts who are outstanding judges of what a certain minor league player's ceiling might be. It's a crapshoot in many instances, but taking a chance on solid young players can often pay huge dividends. If the player is the real thing, it's worth taking the chance. And if the player is ready to play on the major league level right away, a general manager and his scouts can look like geniuses.

Fire Sales

When it comes to making trades, the Grand Old Game has become a high-tech exercise that includes much more than a simple exchange of players that could put your team in a better position to challenge for the pennant. Sadly, there have also been numerous times when the ultimate spot in the standings becomes secondary to the bottom line of the baseball operation, causing organizations to dismantle a successful team strictly for financial reasons. A fire sale is a term that describes a team ridding itself of veteran, talented, more expensive players in exchange for less expensive, often less talented players. When the high-priced, more established players leave a team with financial concerns, they are often replaced with marginal major league talent, draft picks, or prospects who are still unproven on the big-league level.

While such fire sales can help an organization with its profit and loss margins, fans often feel deserted by their team and lose their loyalty to the organization. Recent years have seen numerous examples of such happenings. Few fire sales were as destructive as Wayne Huizenga's dismantling of his world champion Florida Marlins squad following their 1997 championship season.

Citing large financial losses, the Marlins parted ways with

numerous key performers, including Moises Alou, Bobby Bonilla, Kevin Brown, Gary Sheffield, Alex Delgado, Darren Daulton, Robb Nen, Devon White, Jeff Conine, Al Leiter, and Alex Arias. The team plummeted in the standings and disgruntled fans in South Florida coined the phrase, "Wait 'til last year."

It was déjà vu all over again in 2003 as the Marlins once again won the World Series over the New York Yankees. But then over the next two seasons, players such as Derrek Lee, Mark Redman, Brad Penny, Carl Pavano, Ivan Rodriguez, A. J. Burnett, Todd Jones, Antonio Alfonseca, Juan Encarnacion, Carlos Delgado, Paul LoDuca, Mike Lowell, Josh Beckett, and Guillermo Mota were dealt or sold to other clubs.

But try to avoid the temptation to crucify Mr. Huizenga for his actions. The reality is that the Florida franchise is nowhere near the first organization to conduct such house-cleaning fire sales. In the early 1990s, the San Diego Padres decided to call it quits with its current crop of key players. Following a third-place finish in the National League West in 1992, the team let go or traded Randy Myers, Benito Santiago, Tony Fernandez, Darrin Jackson, Gary Sheffield, Rich Rodriguez, Fred McGriff, Bruce Hurst, and Greg Harris. While the team got some talented, young players in exchange, it would not be until 1998 that they became National League champions.

Just north of the border, the Montreal Expos have seen some limited success during the history of that star-crossed franchise. But in the mid-1990s, a talented core of players was handed walking papers and road maps in moves that ultimately condemned major league baseball in Montreal.

Following the strike in 1994 and extending for the next few years, Montreal continually lost good players. Larry Walker, John Wetteland, Ken Hill, Marquis Grissom, Sean Berry, Wil Cordero, Jeff Fassero, Moises Alou, Darrin Fletcher, Mike Lansing, and Pedro Martinez were just some of the All-Star-caliber players who were let go. Needless to say, the Expos could not compete on the playing field and attendance suffered drastically, which led to the team being moved to Washington, D.C., and renamed the Washington Nationals. The quaint days and lovable teams that played at Jarry Park as well as the very competitive Montreal teams who called Olympic Stadium home are now nothing more than a wistful memory. The lovable Expos mascot, Youppi, the French word for hooray, has nothing to cheer for anymore.

Two teams that dominated baseball in the 1970s, the Oakland Athletics and the Cincinnati Reds, cut payroll and started over as their top players began to age. Following the 1976 campaign the onslaught began. Oakland saw Gene Tenace, Rollie Fingers, Sal Bando, Joe Rudi, Don Baylor, Reggie Jackson, Ken Holtzman, and Vida Blue leave town for greener pastures.

In Cincinnati, the Big Red Machine was a distant memory by 1981 and some of the top Reds players left town, including Ray Knight, Ken Griffey Sr., Dave Collins, Tom Seaver, Joe Morgan, Pete Rose, Dave Concepcion, and Johnny Bench.

Try not to judge these franchises too harshly, as the idea of fire sales goes back years and years in the history of baseball. As far back as 1933, the fire sale was part of the landscape of professional baseball. Connie Mack, owner and manager of the Philadelphia Athletics, conducted a fire sale after the 1933 season. Over the next two years, he parted ways with stellar performers such as Mickey Cochrane, George Earnshaw, Lefty Grove, Max Bishop, Rube Walberg, Jimmie Foxx, Al Simmons, Doc Cramer, and Jimmy Dykes.

As a continuation of the self-destructive fire sale, on December 10, 1935, the A's sent the great Foxx and Johnny Marcum to the Boston Red Sox in exchange for Gordon Rhodes, George Savino, and $150,000. Foxx responded with six solid seasons in Boston while Rhodes went 9-20 with a 5.74 ERA in his final major league season. Savino never played in the major leagues.

And when you think about it, the deal that saw the Boston Red Sox send young Babe Ruth to the New York Yankees was also part of a fire sale. In baseball, much as in life, history has a way of repeating itself.

Super Two's, Pre-arbitration, and Arbitration

After a baseball player has fulfilled six years of service with the major league organization that held his rights, the player can declare himself a free agent and can sign with whichever organization he chooses. Before this six-year mark, the player is bound to the organization that controls his rights. Each winter, every major league club must decide whether to offer a contract to each of these pre–free agent players on their 40-man roster. If a team chooses not to offer a contract, that player is then "non-tendered" and immediately becomes a free agent and is free to sign with any organization he chooses. But he still has to complete six full seasons to be free from arbitration rules.

There are three parts to the six-year period: Super Two's, pre-arbitration, and arbitration. Super Two's applies to all players with more than two years of service but less than three. Under the original rules, none of these players were eligible for salary arbitration. But now under the Super Two rules, the top 17 percent of these players by service time also become arbitration eligible. In addition to being in the top 17 percent, the player must also have at least eighty-six days of service time in the immediate preceding season.

During the pre-arbitration years, the organization still holds all the salary control. During the first three years of service time, a player (except a Super Two) has no leverage with the club that controls his rights, much like in the pre–Curt Flood years. Prior to every season, all the organization has to do is offer the player a contract at or near the major league set minimum salary and it retains the player. At the beginning of the new Collective Bargaining Agreement, the 2007 minimum salary became $380,000. In each successive season a player is tendered a contract. During the pre-arbitration years, the team has the option to pay the player the minimum salary set by the league, or give the player a raise over that figure. While players who spend the entire previous year in the major leagues will usually receive a raise, it is not required.

Following three years of service, a player enters the arbitration years, the first real example of the tremendous strides made by the players that have so frustrated ownership. Of course, a player's minimum salary also shows marked improvements over earlier years when players found it necessary to hold down jobs during the off-season. More often than not, major league baseball players are full-time baseball players now.

During the arbitration years, an organization no longer can offer a contract that must be accepted, as in the pre-arbitration years. In the arbitration years, the player has some control over his salary for the next season. During these years, the organization submits a contract offer to the player, who can accept it and sign on the dotted line or decline the offer and submit to the team a salary figure of his own. When that happens, the organization and the player take their case before an arbiter, who decides which salary to award the player. Part of the process used in arbitration includes past arbitration awards given to players of similar service time and ability. The arbiter has to choose either the organization's offer or the player's offer and cannot set any other salary for the player, such as meeting halfway. If the team and player can agree on a contract before the hearing is held, the best possible scenario, the arbitration process ends when the contract is signed.

During the hearing, the player is given one hour to present his case, followed by an hour for the club to present its side. After a break to prepare rebuttals, each side is allowed thirty minutes for rebuttal. The arbitrators then have twenty-four hours to render their decision. There has been at least one occasion when a case was settled after a hearing. In a 1994 case involving the Houston Astros and relief pitcher Tom Edens, the hearing was held with both sides anticipating a decision the following day. However, in the evening after the hearing, the agent for Edens called Bob Watson, then the Houston general manager, and suggested that they settle at the midpoint of the filings. Watson agreed and the arbitrator was relieved of the responsibility of reaching a decision.

The Collective Bargaining Agreement is specific regarding what is admissible and non-admissible in a hearing. Admissible items include the quality of the player's performance, the length and consistency of his performance, his record of past compensation, any physical or mental defects, and comparative baseball salaries. The arbitrators are directed to give particular attention to contracts of players not exceeding one service group above that of the player.

Non-admissible items include the financial position of the player or the club, press comments on the player's performance, and prior offers by either side.

The 10/5 Rule

Even if trades can be agreed upon before the August waiver wire deadline, or during the off-season, the 10/5 rule can also make a general manager's job more difficult. The 10/5 rule, also known as the Curt Flood rule, states that if a player has been on an active major league roster for ten full seasons and on the same team for the last five, that he may not be traded to another team without his consent. In other words, he can veto any deal that he chooses. Many players have negotiated to include no-trade clauses in their contract that have the same effect. Some no-trade clauses are full no-trade, so that it is exactly like the 10/5 rule, with the player having total control over where he will play. Others have negotiated a partial no-trade clause, where they list a number of teams that they will accept a trade to, or cities they will refuse to go to, giving the organization some leverage in making trades.

Free Agents

When a player is offered a contract by his drafting team, or any team he is traded to, each year, he may not become a free agent until he has been on a major league roster or disabled list for at least six years. Otherwise, any player without a contract may become a free agent and sign with any team.

It should be noted that prior to the Curt Flood, Andy Messersmith, and Dave McNally era, there was no such thing as Super Two's, no arbitration, no 10/5 rule, and no free agency. Before that, major league organizations could do pretty much whatever they wanted as far as player transactions were concerned.

Much like the Virginia Slims cigarette commercials of the 1970s, it most certainly could be said of baseball players, "You've come a long way, baby."

THE EARLY YEARS

In a time and place far away from the advent of the new retro-style ballparks that have filled the skyline of baseball today, even the original parks that retro parks copy were not even conceptualized yet. There weren't stadiums, but fields where the boys of summer helped formulate the game of baseball, often dressed in attire that more resembled that of a business meeting than what they called a "base ball" game.

In the early days of base ball, various teams played with different sets of rules, often decided geographically, until the New York Knickerbockers were founded on September 23, 1845. Led by Alexander Cartwright, it was the Knickerbockers who formulated their own rules, making their version of the game closely resemble baseball as we know it today. Fielders would tag or force out base runners, as opposed to the former rule of soaking, or plugging, the runner, in which a fielder could get a runner out by plunking him with the thrown ball. Other Knickerbocker rules included nine-player lineups, ninety-foot base paths, three bases plus home plate, and the diamond-shaped infield that has become so familiar to fans ever since. They played at Elysian Fields in Hoboken, New Jersey, often retiring to a local hotel bar, McCarty's, to discuss the day's diamond events. Some things in the game have changed. Other things, like hoisting a few at a place like McCarty's, remain the same.

The New York style was easier to follow than its rival Massachusetts's game. In the game played by the Knickerbockers' neighbors to the north, there was one out per inning. But under their rules, the winning team was forced to score one hundred runs. Obviously, the Knickerbockers were advocates of speeding up the game.

The allure of baseball soon spread as sixteen clubs composed the National Association of Base Ball Players (NABBP) in 1857. A decade later, more than 400 clubs belonged to the NABBP. That organization morphed into a new league, the National Association of Professional Base Ball Players.

"Initially as early as 1862 to 1864, we begin to see the competition for ballplayers, which was considerable during the Civil War," said baseball historian Jerrold Casway, author of *Ed Delahanty in the Emerald Age of Baseball*. "As baseball became more professional and more competitive, baseball trades became much more frequent. A lot of the better athletes were playing cricket and going into the military to serve in the Civil War. Baseball is a product, I think, of the recreational games of the Civil War. After that, there was a major jump in the game."

The National League was founded in 1875 and is still in existence today, baseball's senior circuit. It awarded teams to cities with a minimum of 75,000 people and enjoyed exclusive territorial rights. The first teams in the league were based in Boston, Chicago, Cincinnati, Hartford, Louisville, New York, Philadelphia, and St. Louis.

"After the war you have a plethora of different teams which created lots of opportunity for anyone with specialized skills at different positions," said Casway. "In the late 1860s, the pre–National Association years, the better players were attracted by jobs and money to major venues like Chicago, New York, and Philadelphia.

Alexander Cartwright defined the game as we know it.
National Baseball Hall of Fame Library, Cooperstown, NY.

You see owners attracting ballplayers by giving them jobs in their own companies and setting them up in business.

"By 1871, it really was professional baseball. With the competition there was the opportunity for free agents. Up until the reserve clause, players had the opportunity to move around. The *Sunday Mercury* newspaper had box scores in it and you could read about the players moving from team to team. They really weren't traded. They simply went to where they felt they could get the best deal. Lipman Pike seemed like he would trade teams every two years [Pike, a left-handed hitting and throwing outfielder, second baseman, and shortstop, routinely changed teams in the 1870s and 1880s, playing for the St. Louis Brown Stockings, Cincinnati Reds, Providence Grays, Worcester Ruby Reds, and the New York Metropolitans.] He was a small guy, about five foot eight, who was a real home run hitter.

"Owners didn't have much say or control of a ballplayer. With the advent of the reserve clause it became a time when owners didn't want to see these players jumping, or revolving to other teams. Up to that point, it was the individual who could call his fate. I believe that at this point, the owners then were able to control the players. If they didn't like a guy, his politics, or thought he was a troublemaker, they could move him. A predominant player like King Kelly could be given part of a trade fee. Players today with their no-trade clauses can negate a trade. But in the old days, a player could be given a kickback. It was a fairly common practice."

A growing problem in the game was players revolving, or jumping from one professional team to another. Player salaries became a huge expense for the teams, most of which failed to make a profit. Club officials felt that the players should help out and share some of the expenses of the day. In fact, players were expected to pay for their uniforms, as well as keep them clean. Boston's Jim O'Rourke jumped to the Providence team due to a dispute over his uniform-upkeep responsibilities.

This infuriated owners, who, at an 1879 meeting, agreed that each team could reserve five players for the following season and that no league team would sign a player reserved by another league team.

Another gathering by representatives of the three major baseball organizations of the day, the National League, the American Association, and the Northwestern League, resulted in the Tripartite Agreement of 1883. The agreement, which was later renamed the National Agreement, cited the need for a central authority to govern the associations. An arbitration committee was formed consisting of three representatives from each organization. When the agreement came into being, each club then had the right to reserve eleven players. The American Association was known as the Beer and Whiskey League, because unlike in the National League, the sale of alcoholic beverages to spectators was allowed. The leagues increased the number of reserved players to fourteen in 1887. That is the same year that the reserve clause was written into a player's contract.

"What the reserve clause brought in was that the players were now controlled," said Casway. "The owners could only get away with that because of the tacit agreement amongst them that they would recognize the rights and responsibilities of each other and they would not violate that. The reserve clause changed the relationship with the ballplayers. The collusion of the owners to protect their investment and property is how they determine the fate of a ballplayer. And in the 1880s, you saw a greater frequency in the movement of the players who were being traded."

The reserve clause stated that upon the contract's expiration, the rights to the player belonged to the team which he had signed with. Even after the typical one-year contract expired, the player was bound to his original club. The player could negotiate a new contract or go home and find a job. There was no free movement of baseball players from the perspective of the player. They were bound to the club they signed their first contract with until they were released, or their contract was sold, or they were traded to a different team. This system stayed in place for nearly one hundred years, until the likes of Curt Flood, Andy Messersmith, Dave McNally, Marvin Miller, and Peter Seitz began to make their ultimate mark on the game and business of baseball.

"What motivated owners to move ballplayers?" asked Jerrold Casway. "First, salary squabbles and resistance to the reserve clause. The player was a troublemaker. Or the age of the ballplayer could be a deciding factor in the decision to make a trade. A lot of older stars of the '80s began to move from team to team through trades. They were huge drawing cards, but the owners did not want to pay large salaries.

"There are also union factors. The owners saw union men as a malignancy. They wanted to break up whatever political cliques they might have had. Troublemakers were part of the dissention factor. An unhappy ballplayer drinks and then shows up drunk. A player like a Dick Allen is perceived as negative. Even back then, the owners had the fate of the player at hand. There simply was not too much a player could do. If a Ned Hanlon decides to move a player, the player does not have to go, but he won't play in that league if he doesn't. Ed Delahanty always threatened to go out and play in California. But they knew he would never do it because they couldn't pay him."

While Delahanty played with the Phillies, he was part of one of the best outfields in major league history, being paired with fellow Hall of Fame members Sam Thompson and Sliding Billy Hamilton. All three players hit over .400 in 1894, another memorable accomplishment of note. When former manager Harry Wright passed away on October 3, 1895, the Phillies organization hesitated in bringing back manager Art Irwin, despite his two-year managerial record of 149-110. When no commitment was made, Irvin decided to manage in New York. He was replaced by Billy Shettsline, an employee of the club with no major league playing experience. While he was not expected to be manager-of-the-year material, his major function was to keep the team running smoothly. But his hiring forced the team to search for an on-field captain to help run the club and make game decisions.

In order to secure the services of third baseman Billy Nash, a competent player and great field general from the Boston Bean-eaters, Philadelphia traded one third of its Cooperstown-bound outfield, Billy Hamilton. Sliding Billy Hamilton got that moniker because he revolutionized the game by inventing the head-first slide, the drag bunt, and going from first to third on a single. The speedy runner set a record by stealing seven bases in a single game

Billy Hamilton was an innovative base runner and the first New Jersey Hall of Famer.
National Baseball Hall of Fame Library, Cooperstown, NY.

on August 31, 1894. After his trade to Boston, Hamilton continued his fine play, hitting over .300 in five of the six seasons he played for the Beaneaters. He was the first native of New Jersey elected to the Hall of Fame.

The Phillies did not fare nearly as well with Nash, whose career was drastically affected after he was hit in the head with a pitched ball.

"When the Phillies traded Billy Hamilton, they wanted a guy who could help them play the Orioles style of play," said Caswell. "They went out and got Billy Nash from the Beaneaters. It was a huge trade that did not work out for the Phillies. A couple of years later, they actually moved about four players who were known as drinkers to St. Louis. That was something you didn't see every day. The Phillies wanted to break up this hard-drinking clique."

In addition to behavior issues and debates over temperance, the acrimony over the reserve clause was felt right from the start. An interesting character of the game in that era was John Montgomery Ward, a Hall of Fame pitcher and shortstop, who played for seventeen years with Providence, New York, and Brooklyn. Monte Ward hit a solid .275 during his career and also boasted a 164-102 mark as a hurler. Ward pitched the second perfect game in the history of baseball on June 17, 1880, as a member of the Providence Grays, retiring all twenty-seven Buffalo batters in a 5-0 win.

Just four days earlier, John Lee Richmond of Worcester threw the first perfect game in history, beating Cleveland, 1-0. During that contest, Worcester right fielder Lon Knight preserved the gem when he gunned down Silver Bill Phillips of Cleveland before he reached first base on what appeared to be a clean, hard-hit single. Monte Ward's perfect game was the last in the National League until eighty-four years later when Jim Bunning of the Philadelphia Phillies threw a perfecto against the New York Mets on Father's Day of 1964, en route to a 6-0 victory.

Monte Ward helped form the first players' union when he, Ned Hanlon, and others began the Brotherhood of Professional Base-

Union activist John Montgomery Ward hurled baseball's second perfecto.
National Baseball Hall of Fame Library, Cooperstown, NY.

ball Players in 1885. In articles written in the late 1880s, Ward had harsh words for the reserve clause, calling it, "a conspiracy, pure and simple, on the part of the clubs by which they are making money rightfully belonging to the players." A short time later, they challenged the reserve clause and actually negotiated a compromise with the owners, guaranteeing that the reserve clause could not be used to bind a player to a team while his salary was being cut. The owners also put aside their $2,000 salary cap.

The victory for the players was short-lived, as just one year later, in the winter of 1888, while Ward and other Brotherhood leaders were on a world tour with Albert Spalding's Chicago White Sox, the National League owners met and adopted a grading system which would seriously threaten a player's earning potential. This was established to create a fixed scale of salaries for the players. There was a five-step salary classification scale which set the top wage at $2,500. The grading system and the way in which the owners turned their backs on the previous year's agreement outraged Ward and other players to the point that they organized their own rival league, the Players League, which was controlled by the players. But the league folded after just one season and Ward returned to finish out his career in the National League as a player/manager.

At the age of thirty-four, Ward retired at the conclusion of the 1894 season to pursue his law career, but continued to be a thorn in the side of ownership. When Giants owner Andrew Freedman let go veteran infielder Fred Pfeffer for being "an old stiff," Ward represented Pfeffer in court and won the player his salary for the season. Incidentally, Pfeffer is credited with being the first infielder to cut off a catcher's throw to second base on a double steal attempt and throw out the runner trying to score from third base.

It was also during 1894 that the Western League, which had been founded eleven years before, began to make a name for itself under the leadership of Ban Johnson, a former sports writer for the *Cincinnati Commercial-Gazette*. The Western League was renamed the American League and Johnson, along with his friend, former Cincinnati executive Charlie Comiskey, saw their upstart league gain parity with the National League. In January of 1901, at a meeting at the Chicago Grand Pacific Hotel, the American League declared itself a major league and planned a 140-game schedule for the upcoming season.

Their dedication to building a successful new league with the best players available caused severe turmoil in the National League.

Existing teams included Chicago, Cleveland, Detroit, and Milwaukee. New American League franchises were awarded to Baltimore, Boston, and Philadelphia. The team in Kansas City was transferred to the nation's capital.

Serious bidding for top players continued. Philadelphia Phillies infielder Napoleon "Nap" Lajoie attempted to jump to the Phils' crosstown rival, the American League Athletics. But a court injunction barred Lajoie from playing in Pennsylvania, so he was traded to Cleveland, where he enjoyed some of the best years of his stellar career.

The bidding war between the two "major" leagues caused a meeting in Chicago in September of 1901 which resulted in the formation of the National Association of Professional Baseball Leagues. This new association protected the National and American leagues from any future Ban Johnsons who had designs on the top players of the two leagues. The following year, both leagues signed an agreement which reinforced the power of the reserve clause and ended the stealing of players. The agreement also established a system of control for the major leagues over upstart independent leagues.

A major benefit of the 1901 meeting was the understanding that in 1903, the NL would have its pennant winner play a World Series against the AL champion. The new kids on the block did well from the start as Boston, of the American League, won the inaugural World Series. But what this agreement also did was allow the major leagues to reign over the independent leagues, basically allowing them a monopoly in professional baseball. A three-man body was created by the National Agreement, the National Commission, which took over control of professional baseball. The commission had papal-like power concerning its interpretation of the terms and provisions of the National Agreement. It also had the power to levy fines and suspensions. This body ruled baseball until 1921, when the position of commissioner of baseball was formed in response to the 1919 Black Sox scandal.

"Once the leagues came together and did a new national agreement, the lawsuits were dropped," said Casway. "At that point Lajoie was allowed to play in Pennsylvania. And with the agreements, the reserve clause was strong and the national agreement was in place, giving owners dominance over the careers of their players. Up until 1920 there was a silver age of baseball with two leagues, the National and the American, that controlled everything. They paid the top salaries, had the collusion and had the control."

Player transactions became commonplace in the game, but not in the form that is known in today's game. The first transaction on record was in 1873 when Mansfield's Jim O'Rourke signed with the Boston Red Stockings as a free agent. For the next twelve years player movement involved similar free agent signings, players being purchased for cash, and of course, players being released. In 1875, the Philadelphia Athletics purchased George Bechtel, an outfielder and pitcher, from the Philadelphia Centennials for a mere $1,500. That purchase price was considerably more than what the Chicago White Stockings received in exchange for Hugh Nicol in 1883, when the St. Louis Browns paid just $50 to acquire the light-hitting utility infielder and outfielder.

The first actual player exchange on record occurred on August 29, 1885, when Chattanooga sent Toad Ramsey to the Louisville Colonels for John Connor and $750, as two young pitchers changed teams. While Connor would have just a 2-8 big league record, Ramsey went 114-124 in his six-year career. In the midst of an 8-30 season with Louisville in 1888, Ramsey purposely missed a team train to avoid being arrested due to a complaint from a Louisville saloon owner who charged that Ramsey failed to pay a considerable bar tab.

In November of 1886, the Cincinnati Red Stockings dealt Jack Boyle and $350 to the St. Louis Browns for Hugh Nicol, whose stock had risen considerably since being traded for $50, just three years earlier. A month later, the Pittsburgh Alleghenys traded Otto Schomberg and $400 to the St. Louis Maroons in exchange for Alex McKinnon.

It seems that the art of making the baseball trade was changing with every transaction and was being made up along the way. The owners controlled the game to a large degree and players were mere pawns in the chess game of baseball.

"The first great era of trades in the 1890s, the situation was that it was all one sided," said Jerrold Casway. "Until the founding of the American League, which entices Ed Delahanty and Nap Lajoie, there was simply no leverage for the players. You had real collusion because all the players are bound by the reserve clause and the national agreement. The owners had a monopolistic control over the players."

That control enjoyed by the owners didn't end with the control over their team and players. This was the time in the history of the game when trades were made to improve a ball club, rid the team of a troublemaker, or in certain instances, increase the leverage enjoyed by ownership.

The end of the nineteenth century also marked what is viewed as a dark time in the history of the game, when owners who had financial interests in more than one team made decisions that ended proud franchises, while padding the wallets of the owners who saw more profit in different cities.

Take, for instance, the strange case that involved two franchises and one owner. Just before the turn of the century in 1899, Louisville Colonels owner Barney Dreyfus knew that his team was one of the clubs that would be contracted, or eliminated from the league following that season. The total number of teams was being reduced from twelve to eight. So Dreyfus, with some real insider trader information at his fingertips, engineered a trade from one team he partly owned, Louisville, to another team he partly owned, the Pittsburgh Pirates.

On December 12, 1899, Dreyfus of Louisville sent Honus Wagner, Rube Waddell, Fred Clarke, Mike Kelley, Patsy Flaherty, Deacon Phillippe, Icebox Chamberlain, Walt Woods, Chief Zimmer, Conny Doyle, Tom Massitt, Tommy Leach, Tacks Latimer, and Claude Ritchey to his Pittsburgh Pirates club in exchange for Jack Chesbro, Paddy Fox, John O'Brien, Art Madison, and $25,000.

It can't even be said that Dreyfus acted dishonestly. Multi-ownership was not banned by baseball until 1910, so the astute Dreyfus was acting clearly in his own best interest and not outside of the laws of the game.

Barney Dreyfus was not the only owner to desert a city that had supported his team. Robert Irsay and the Baltimore Colts had plenty of precedence. The Cleveland Spiders were a very successful team in the 1890s, sporting such great players as Cy Young, Jesse Burkett, and Bobby Wallace. The team was owned by two brothers, Frank and Stanley Robison. Prior to the inception of the World Series in 1903, the equivalent to the Fall Classic was the Temple Cup. And the Robison brothers' Spiders were the Temple Cup champions in 1895.

The following season, the Cleveland nine were runners up in the Temple Cup sweepstakes. But then the club had consecutive subpar fifth-place finishes. However, compared to what was about to happen in 1899, those two second-division placements must have seemed like the Temple Cup championship all over again. It was during spring training of 1899 when Young, Burkett, Wallace, and virtually all of the best Spider players were traded to St. Louis, another team that the Robison brothers just happened to have ownership in.

Frank and Stanley Robison had a proud tradition in Cleveland, a city known for its moral fiber. St. Louis was also a fine city, populated by good people who loved Sunday baseball and beer. After seeing attendance drop at League Park in Cleveland from 150,000 a year to a mere 70,000 in 1898, the Brothers Robison were certain that the answer to their attendance woes was the institution of Sunday baseball, something that the city of Cleveland was just not ready for.

So while the Robisons flirted with the idea of moving to another city such as Buffalo or Rochester, a number of situations made their path to St. Louis incredibly clear. With slumping attendance, the Spiders were forced by their owners to play home games on the road, in such venues as Rochester and Weehawken, New Jersey. While the team had a legitimate shot at the pennant until the middle of August, the strain of constant travel took its toll. The great Cy Young said, "We could have won it by playing all our games at home."

It was at this point that fate intervened in favor of the Robisons. The St. Louis franchise was a mess, thanks to an underachieving team and a poorly maintained park that actually had been damaged by a fire. But through it all, the Browns enjoyed a very loyal, interested fan base that supported the last-place club. The Robisons saw St. Louis, and rightly so, as a place that would draw more fans to the games. Plus, Frank Robison was not a supporter of Cleveland fans. During a labor dispute, he had hired non-union workers to operate his streetcar company, which caused some unions to boycott the Spiders.

Over the winter, the rest of the league's owners, along with the governing body of St. Louis, worked to remove the owner of the Browns, brewer Chris van der Ahe, from his club. He was bought out for $33,000 and one day later the team was purchased by

Frank and Stanley Robison for $40,000, during spring training, 1899.

Beginning just before opening day and lasting throughout the season, they transferred various Cleveland players to St. Louis, including Young, Frank Bates, Lave Cross, Jack Harper, and Charlie Hemphill.

The Spiders won their first game of the season in fourteen innings. But as a result of the onslaught to their roster, the Spiders team of 1899 became what is to this day the worst club in the history of Major League Baseball. They finished what was to be their final season with a record of 20-134. They lost forty of their final forty-one games and finished eighty-four games out of first place. In fact, they were thirty-five games out of next-to-last place.

Consequently, other teams refused to travel to Cleveland's park due to abysmal attendance. The Spiders were forced to play the final thirty-six games of the season on the road, losing all but one. Some of the records of futility they sent will go on in baseball perpetuity, such as 109 road losses in a single season. In today's game, teams only play eighty-one regular season road games. Their longest winning streak of the season was just two games, a trick they accomplished on May 20 and 21.

Some of their players included pitcher Harry "The Pitching Vegetable" Colliflower, who had a 1-11 record. He lost one "nailbiter" to Washington, 31-4, being charged with twenty of the Senators' runs. The Pitching Vegetable and the other hurlers threw to Ossee Schreckengost, who would later become a roommate of Hall of Fame pitcher Rube Wadell. Schreckengost was a workhorse, at one point catching eighteen games in eleven days. He was also known as baseball's pie-eating champion.

While he hit a mediocre .238, shortstop Harry Lochhead was even more of a liability on the field, where he committed eighty-one errors.

Their two winningest pitchers were Jim "Cold Water" Hughey (4-30) and Charlie Knepper (4-22). If a game was going particularly badly, Jim "Cold Water" Hughey would occasionally just sit down on the pitcher's mound to take a break. Knepper had a heart of gold, completing all twenty-six games he started. During the course of their thirty-four home games, just 6,088 fans paid to see the Spiders go 9-25 in Cleveland. The paltry average attendance in 1899 was just 179 per game.

But even in the darkest of circumstances, sometimes an interesting and heartwarming sidebar can occur. Cleveland manager Joe Quinn had befriended a nineteen-year-old worker at a cigar stand, Eddie Kolb. Upon hearing Quinn complain that his scheduled starter for the final game of the year was ill, Kolb convinced Quinn to let him pitch the season finale against Cincinnati. Kolb pitched a complete game, allowing nineteen runs on eighteen hits in a losing effort.

After his lone major league appearance, Eddie Kolb managed a pennant-winning team in the Ohio State League in 1902 and the next year managed the Huntington, West Virginia, club to the High River Valley League championship. After a successful stint as an outfielder/manager with Vincennes, of the Kitty League, he played left field and was the skipper of the Brockton team in the New England League.

Financially successful, Kolb just failed in an attempt to buy the Montreal franchise in 1908 before embarking on a long and prosperous career in the petroleum industry. But up until his death in 1948, Eddie Kolb fondly treasured the memory of his lone major league appearance.

After his baseball life, manager Joe Quinn became an undertaker. After all, he certainly understood loss. But in spite of the carnage that the Robison brothers inflicted on Cleveland and the Spiders, it wasn't long before Ban Johnson came calling, which led to the formation of the Cleveland Indians of the American League.

Even the 1962 New York Mets, who stumbled to a 40-120 record, and the 2003 Detroit Tigers, with their 43-119 mark, don't really come close to the atrocious 20-134 example of futility that led to the end of the once-proud Cleveland Spiders club.

The same scenario occurred in Baltimore, where a strong Orioles club, led by manager Ned Hanlon, finished in first place from 1894 to 1896. Hanlon's nine were on the cutting edge of the game, making strategies such as the hit-and-run and fielders cutting off throws a regular part of baseball that was then widely imitated. But owner Harry Vonderhorst also had interests in the Brooklyn Superbas team and felt that attendance would be higher in Brooklyn. So he began systematically sending his better players and manager Hanlon to New York, much like a large company would transfer employees from one city to another.

The result was that the Superbas won pennants in 1899 and 1900, while the Orioles folded following that season. As alluded to earlier, situations such as these where individuals or groups own more than one club were rather common in baseball's early years. But owning more than one club, known as syndicalism, is no longer allowed.

Baseball trades, not simply signings, continued to occur with more regularity in the early years of the twentieth century, as the game entered what is known as the dead ball era. Pitching was the name of the game and miserly owners would often use a single baseball for an entire game, no matter how dirty, dark, or dingy it may have become. Some owners had guards who would retrieve baseballs that left the field of play.

Many of the most famous pitchers in the history of baseball toiled in this era, including the likes of Cy Young, Rube Waddell, "Iron Man" Joe McGinnity, Christy Mathewson, Eddie Plank, Big Ed Walsh, Grover Cleveland Alexander, "Smokey Joe" Wood, and Walter "Big Train" Johnson. That's not to say that these masters of the mound would not have been successful with baseballs that could be seen after the early innings, but hitters were at a distinct disadvantage during this time.

Disadvantage turned to tragedy on August 16, 1920, when

Cleveland's Ray Chapman was killed with a pitched ball. The Yankees' starter that day was Carl Mays, a hard-throwing, side-wheeling spitball specialist. Mays was on the mound for New York as Ray Chapman stepped up to the plate to lead off the inning.

Mays was known as a mean pitcher who would quite often dust a batter off with inside pitches. Chapman was a scrappy player who crowded the plate in a crouched stance and was often hit by pitches. But as he led off the inning, it was felt that Chapman was possibly expecting Mays to start him off with a breaking ball away. But Mays threw his first pitch of the at bat high and inside, literally freezing Chapman, who never moved away from the pitch. He was hit on the left side of his head and the sound of the impact of the baseball resonated throughout the Polo Grounds. Of course, in 1920, batting helmets were not used. Blood ran out of his ears, mouth, and nose.

As medical personnel and teammates rushed to his aid, Chapman lay unconscious on the ground. He was revived, however, and tried to walk off the field into the dugout, but began to collapse and was carried off the field by his Indian teammates.

X-rays at the hospital showed that Chapman had suffered a depressed fracture of the left side of the skull. His condition grew steadily worse throughout the evening and surgery was performed just after midnight, even though Chapman's wife had not yet arrived in New York. The hour-long procedure saw surgeons remove a piece of the player's skull during the operation. Although the immediate response to the surgery was encouraging, Ray Chapman died at 4:40 a.m. on August 17, 1920.

As a result of the tragic death of Ray Chapman, baseball made some changes to the basic way the game was played. The established tradition of using the same baseball, often for an entire game, ended. Now new balls were used and dirty or scoffed baseballs were replaced and no longer used. This made the ball much easier for batters to see, particularly at twilight.

A new law also made it illegal for a pitcher to doctor the baseball, making pitches such as the spitball, shineball, and greaseball illegal. Since quite a few pitchers relied on those pitches as their primary weapon, the law was grandfathered in so that hurlers who depended on the spitball were allowed to finish their careers still using that pitch. The last pitcher to earn a victory in the major league throwing a legal spitball was the Pittsburgh Pirates' Burleigh Grimes, in 1934.

Finally, in spite of the tragic death of Ray Chapman, it was eleven seasons before a Major League Baseball player wore a batting helmet at the plate. On March 7, 1941, Pee Wee Reese and Joe Medwick of the Brooklyn Dodgers wore batting helmets. Ironically, on that historic day, the Dodgers beat Ray Chapman's old team, the Cleveland Indians, 15-0.

With the emphasis on pitching in baseball's dead ball era, a new name began to circulate in baseball circles. There was a talented young left-handed pitcher from an orphanage in Baltimore who would probably have the most profound effect on the game of any player before or since. His name was George Herman Ruth. He is most famous for his incredible years as a member of the New York Yankees. But while the trade of the Bambino from Boston to New York is one of the most famous, as well as infamous, deals in baseball history, there were opportunities for other teams to acquire Ruth early in his career.

In fairness to the Boston Red Sox, who endured the Curse of the Bambino, other teams, including the Athletics and Phillies, very possibly could have had Babe Ruth in their starting lineup. In reality, the Curse extended well beyond Beantown.

Any student of the game would be hard-pressed to find a deal that resonated throughout the game more than the sale of George Herman "Babe" Ruth from the Boston Red Sox to the New York Yankees. It could also be argued that the Boston Red Sox were in the midst of a fire sale when they traded the Big Bambino to the New York Yankees.

No matter how you look at it, that transaction was the blockbuster of all blockbusters.

2

THE CURSE OF THE BAMBINO

A Blockbuster of a Fire Sale

While young George Ruth was growing up in Baltimore, he spent much of his childhood in St. Mary's Industrial School. While it is often referred to as an orphanage, or reform school, it was actually a training school for orphans, delinquents, and children from broken homes and poor families who could not afford to raise them or help them get an education.

In later years, Ruth would often speak of the person he called the greatest man he ever knew, Brother Matthias, of the Roman Catholic Xaverian Brothers, who was his mentor at St. Mary's. While Brother Matthias was trying to trim some of young George's rough edges, he also saw that Ruth had exceptional baseball skills and spent countless hours teaching him the game of baseball. As the years passed, George always played baseball with older boys and still managed to excel.

Ruth actually wanted to be a catcher, but was soon to learn that even in those days, left-handed catchers were not part of the game and left-handed catchers' mitts did not even exist. Today, a statue of Ruth stands at the Eutaw Street entrance of Camden Yards in

Baltimore which shows him holding a catcher's mitt for a left-handed-throwing player. That is not a mistake; it is a true representation of a young Ruth.

He eventually became a pitcher who could also hit the ball a country mile. Baseball was still in the midst of the dead ball era and as a result there was always a keen eye out for young pitching prospects. That's just what Ruth was.

Just a week before the young pitcher turned nineteen, Jack Dunn, owner and manager of the Baltimore Orioles of the International League, signed George Ruth to his first baseball contract for $600 on February 14, 1914. Minor league teams in that era made money by developing young players who could then be sold to major league clubs. A former major league pitcher and infielder, Dunn knew a "can't miss" prospect when he saw one.

In his autobiography, *The Babe Ruth Story*, by Ruth and Bob Considine, the Bambino told of his excitement over his first contract.

"I had some great moments in the years that followed that, including the day I signed a contract for $80,000 a year with the New York Yankees. But none of my later thrills ever topped the one I got that cold afternoon at St. Mary's when $600 a year seemed to me to be all the wealth in the world."

It was that year during his first spring training in Fayetteville, North Carolina, that Ruth got his nickname, "Babe." While Ruth was having fun playing with an elevator at a hotel, he nearly had his head crushed. The incident was witnessed by numerous teammates who also saw Dunn ream the youngster out. During his loud and pointed discussion with Ruth, Dunn said, "You're just a babe in the woods." From that day forward, he was known as Babe Ruth.

Ruth had some immediate success with Baltimore, earning his first professional victory on April 22 with a six-hit shutout over Buffalo. But that success was dwarfed by the impact of the rival Federal League, another self-proclaimed major league, which

Babe Ruth—the best thing that ever happened to the game.
National Baseball Hall of Fame Library, Cooperstown, NY.

placed a team in Baltimore, the Terrapins. The new team in town drew nearly all of the baseball fans in 1914, often pulling in close to 20,000 fans to a game while the Orioles often drew only hundreds of fans. While Jack Dunn had assembled one of the most talented teams in the International League, sporting a 47-22 record on July 4, the correspondingly large minor league payroll caused his organization to often lose in excess of $2,000 per week.

A number of teams from various leagues had noticed young Babe Ruth. In June of 1914, the Brooklyn club of the Federal League reportedly offered Ruth $30,000 over two years to jump to the new league. But Dunn, who became Ruth's legal guardian upon signing his first contract, would let his young pitcher have nothing to do with the new league that was costing him thousands of dollars.

It was not only the upstart Federal League that began to take notice of Ruth. The Yankees offered $25,000 to Jack Dunn in exchange for Ruth and three other players, but the offer was turned down. Had the Yanks come up with more money, it is possible that Babe Ruth would have been a Yankee beginning in 1914.

Other major league clubs interested in acquiring Ruth included the Giants, Reds, and Braves. In past years Dunn enjoyed a successful relationship selling players to Connie Mack of the Philadelphia Athletics. To some it seemed a certainty that Ruth would become a member of the defending world champion Athletics. Dunn offered both Ruth and another top pitcher, Ernie Shore, to the Athletics. But even though the team was comfortably in first place, Mack passed on the two young hurlers, explaining that he was not in a position to buy due to financial constraints.

The Baltimore Orioles and the Philadelphia A's were not the only teams suffering financially in 1914. The other major league club in Philadelphia, the Phillies, was also suffering due in part to the defection of some of its top players to the Federal League. After Connie Mack turned down the Orioles' offer of Babe Ruth and Ernie Shore, Jack Dunn then offered those two players along with shortstop Claud Derrick to the Phillies for $19,000.

According to Phillies manager Red Dooin, club president William F. Baker was not interested in spending any money to acquire good, young talent.

"Baker nearly exploded when I reported to him that Dunn asked $19,000 for three of the most promising players in the International League," Dooin said. "He told me he wouldn't give $19,000 for the whole International League."

The Orioles' fire sale began in Baltimore on July 7 when they sent outfielder Birdie Cree to New York for $8,000. The next day, shortstop Claud Derrick and outfielder George Twombly were sold to the Cincinnati Reds for $15,000. After that, the fire sale became a blockbuster.

On the following day, July 9, 1914, Ruth was dealt to the Boston Red Sox along with Shore and catcher Ben Egan for an amount of money that is believed to be $18,000.

Ruth had spent only five months with the Orioles before he was sold to the Boston Red Sox. During his first three seasons in Boston, Ruth was primarily a pitcher. After joining the Bosox, Ruth was used sparingly and had a 1-1 record before being sent to Providence to gain experience and help the Grays in a tough pennant race.

In his first full major league season, Ruth boasted an 18-8 record on a talented Red Sox pitching staff that included the likes of Rube Foster and Smokey Joe Wood. Boston won the American League pennant and went on to beat the Phillies, four games to one, in the World Series. It was during the 1915 season that the Babe hit his first four home runs.

Ruth improved to 23-12 in 1916 with a sparkling 1.75 ERA and nine shutouts, a record which still stands today. Once again, Boston won the World Series four games to one, this time against the Brooklyn Robins. In 1917, Boston finished out of postseason play, thanks in large part to a hundred-win season by the Chicago White Sox. But Ruth finished the year with a 24-13 record.

Boston returned to prominence in 1918, winning the World Series over the Chicago Cubs. It was to be the last Red Sox World Series championship for another eighty-four years. It was also in 1918 that the Babe began to view himself as more of a power-hitting outfielder than a pitcher. He was 13-7 on the mound with another good ERA of 2.22, but also hit .300 and led the league with eleven home runs.

The 1919 season was a difficult summer in Boston. The Red Sox had a dismal season, finishing 66-71. Ruth began to beg out of his starting assignments for what were considered questionable maladies. He still managed to sport a 9-5 record. But he also played the outfield and hit .322 with the new single-season home run record of twenty-nine, while driving in 114 runs. The Babe broke the old homer record of twenty-seven, set by Ned Williamson.

Following the 1919 season, Babe Ruth would pitch only five more times in his entire career. It should be noted that he was 5-0 with two complete games. Although he sported an impressive 94-46 record on the mound with an ERA of 2.28, Ruth insisted on becoming an everyday ballplayer at almost the same time that baseball's live ball era began. Babe had good timing. But his talent as a pitcher is sometimes forgotten. There are those who insist that he was well on his way to a Hall of Fame career on the mound. In the World Series, he pitched 29 2/3 scoreless innings, breaking Christy Mathewson's record and setting a mark that would stand for forty-three years.

While his Red Sox team suffered on the playing field in 1919, owner Harry Frazee was undergoing serious financial difficulties. Even though the Boston franchise was the toast of the American League with its star-studded lineup, that lineup and the salaries paid to the players led to other challenges. Success did not come cheaply and the team's huge payroll was made even more difficult to handle because of abysmal attendance due to World War I. In addition to owning the Red Sox, Frazee was a theatre aficionado who had produced a number of Broadway hits. But he was also losing money on several shows he had financed, once again, largely due to the war.

It was at the height of this distressing time that Frazee had a contract dispute with Ruth. The Babe had signed a three-year contract for $10,000 per year, but following his monster 1919 campaign, he demanded $20,000 per year, threatening to sit out the 1920 season if necessary to have his demands met. Frazee was between a rock and a hard place with few options available to him.

Because of his affinity for the theatre, Frazee had an office that was a short walk from the New York Yankees' office, where his old friend, Tillinghast L'Hommedieu Huston, was co-owner of the Yankees with Jacob Ruppert, a millionaire brewer. Ruth commented in his autobiography that he felt he was traded over a few glasses of beer between Huston and Frazee.

Regardless, on January 3, 1920, Frazee sold Ruth to the Yankees in exchange for $125,000 cash and a loan of more than $300,000, which was secured by Fenway Park. On the same day that his team acquired Babe Ruth, Jacob Ruppert, the brewer, lost his fight in the United States Supreme Court to legalize the manufacture and sale of 2.75 percent beer. Clearly on that day, Jacob Ruppert was batting a cool .500 and the Curse of the Bambino was born.

Two days after dealing Ruth, Harry Frazee had this to say about the transaction. "It would be impossible to start next season with Ruth and have a smooth-working machine. Ruth had become simply impossible, and the Boston club could no longer put up with his eccentricities. I think the Yankees are taking a gamble. While Ruth is undoubtedly the greatest hitter the game has ever seen, he is likewise one of the most selfish and inconsiderate men ever to put on a baseball uniform."

To say that the relationship between Babe Ruth and Harry Frazee had deteriorated is an understatement. In an interview with the *New York Times* in the days after the trade, Ruth spoke of his Red Sox days: "I have always hustled as hard as any man on the diamond. When not taking my turn in the box, I played in the outfield, doing everything I could to make the club win. I don't like to play for Frazee. I like Boston and Boston fans. They have treated me splendidly and if it were not for Frazee, I would be content to play with the Red Sox to the end of my baseball days. Frazee sold me because he was unwilling to meet my demands and to alibi himself with the fans he is trying to throw the blame on me."

It has long been felt that Frazee sold Ruth in order to finance a well-known Broadway show, *No, No, Nanette.* However, that show was not to appear until five years later, in 1925. While the sale of Ruth and others may have helped with some of the planning for the popular musical, the direct line from Ruth to Nanette is cloudy at best. A more likely scenario is that the sale of the players enabled Frazee to keep his head above water until he sold the team for $1.25 million in 1923. It was two years later that the famed musical appeared on Broadway.

The impact of the trade makes it both a part of a fire sale as well as a blockbuster. After parting with Ruth, the Red Sox fell on hard times. From 1920 to 1934, the remainder of Ruth's playing days, the Bosox finished in last place ten times and never had a winning season. In fact, it would be eighty-four years until they were able to finally put an end to the Curse of the Bambino by winning the World Series in 2004.

As for the Bronx Bombers, things were much more successful; they reached the World Series seven times and were victorious in four of the Fall Classics. They also got a little lucky, as the Black Sox scandal and the tragic death of Cleveland shortstop Ray Chapman, on August 17, 1920, put an end to the dead ball era, which just happened to coincide with the development of Ruth as a power hitter.

As the dead ball era ended, it was Babe Ruth who helped resuscitate the game after the devastating effects of the death of Chapman in August of 1920 and the admission with a week remaining in that season by Eddie Cicotte, Shoeless Joe Jackson, and Lefty Williams of their part in the Black Sox fix of the World Series the previous year. As Judge Kenesaw Mountain Landis was named the first commissioner of baseball, with absolute power over both owners and players, the best thing that could have happened to the game was Babe Ruth.

His ability is legendary, but the baseball gods also aided in making him the marquee player of his era. Some of the rule changes as well as the manufacture of baseballs that may have been more apt to travel farther than those in previous years all helped make Babe Ruth the Sultan of Swat and the New York Yankees forever to be thought of as trading geniuses.

Home run records fell by the wayside as Ruth rewrote the record books, often hitting more homers himself than entire teams did. He was a lovable character on and off the field and was one of the most popular players in the game, held in high esteem by opponents and teammates alike. While the Big Bambino quickly became the most feared hitter in the game with the Yankees, opposing players not only respected his ability, but looked forward to seeing how they could match up against such a dynamic player.

In an interview with *Baseball Magazine* published in 1923, one of the best pitchers of the day, St. Louis Browns right-hander Urban Shocker, gave his thoughts about pitching to Babe Ruth.

"I like to pitch to Babe Ruth better than to anybody else in baseball. And I consider him the most dangerous of all batters.

"Why do I like to pitch to Babe? Because he is a never-ending puzzle. You always have to extend yourself to the utmost when you face Babe. Sometimes he looks very easy, but there is one thing it is never safe for a pitcher to bank on. Any time he figures that he has Babe's number he is feeding himself a liberal dose of misplaced confidence.

"There is one thing that Babe can always be counted upon to supply. He gives the opposing pitcher a thrill no matter what happens. If you strike him out you can get a very pleasurable thrill, as long as it lasts. If he hits you for a solid smash you get another kind of thrill. Why do cowboys ride wild steers and risk their necks on bucking broncos? It's a dangerous sport but it gives them a thrill, I suppose, to think they have conquered something which was strong and reckless and hard to handle."

No matter what he may have accomplished on the playing field, once the game ended, it was over. The Babe rarely spoke about baseball and was a very good and supportive teammate and friend.

"He was a very likable guy," said Bill Werber, who played eleven major league seasons with five teams and is the last living teammate of both Babe Ruth and Lou Gehrig. "Babe was happy wherever he was, a real good, natural sort of fellow. He always acted like a gentleman."

Seven hundred and fourteen home runs later, who can argue that fact?

3

IT TAKES TWO TO TANGO

Just how a baseball trade is made has as many variables as the number of trades that are made. Each trade is unique, made for different reasons. If your team has a hole that can only be filled by Player A from another team, in a perfect baseball world, you have an excess at a certain position where Player A's team has a weakness. At times a player has become a bad influence, become bitter toward management, or simply worn out his welcome on a particular team and needs a change of scenery, allowing a club to add by subtraction.

There are also times when a player simply cannot deal with the pressure of playing for a particular team. Such was the case during pitcher Ed Whitson's short tenure as a member of the New York Yankees. And then there is always a young ballplayer with "can't miss" potential who makes a veteran suddenly available, such as when Ryan Howard supplanted veteran Jim Thome at first base in Philadelphia.

No matter what might be the impetus of making a deal, there are truths of the trade that have held through generation after generation of trading players. While each organization and general manager certainly has different ways of approaching player transactions, Bing Devine, the late long-time general manager, explained the process in his book, *The Memoirs of Bing Devine.*

"You win some, you lose some . . . and sometimes you get lucky," he wrote. "But you don't get lucky if you don't take the chance. That leads to my four tricks for a trade.

"1. You've got to need the player. 2. You've got to have good reports from your scouts and talent evaluators. 3. You've got to have the guts to make the deal. 4. You've got to get lucky.

"But if you never have the guts to do anything, you'll never get lucky. You'll never give yourself the chance to be lucky."

As has often been the case, you have to be good to be lucky and you have to be lucky to be good. Such absolutely is the case when trading baseball players. After all, nothing is guaranteed. Players are traded in much the same way that they are compensated, in part for past performance and in part for future promise. But how often has a prospect turned into a suspect? And how often have trades that made so much sense on paper simply not worked out for one or both of the clubs involved? No matter how much study, evaluation, and scouting a team might do, in many cases it is still a crapshoot. A pitcher can have an MRI on his throwing arm before a trade is made and get a clean bill of health. Two months later he might need Tommy John surgery.

In the golden age of baseball, this complicated maze of trades seemed much simpler as there were no long-term contracts, no-trade clauses, or multi-million-dollar buyouts to contend with. More often than not, a trade was made to improve the ball club. What a concept.

"The nature of the game has really changed," said Tal Smith, president of baseball operations for the Houston Astros. "Today, many more people are involved. You get involved with contract and control issues. As a result of Andy Messersmith and Dave McNally, you have serious control issues now. Before that, you were just talking about talent. Today, a lot more is involved. For instance, is the player arbitration-eligible? Will he be a free agent at the end of the year? Are there specific provisions of his contract that you need to be aware of? As a result of all these variables, there are many more people involved today as opposed to the days when general managers would just make a deal.

"I remember back in 1976, I was at a meeting sitting across from Bing Devine, of St. Louis. He slipped me a note that said he was looking for pitching and asked if we would be willing to trade Larry Dierker. We consummated the deal at the first recess by trading Larry to the Cardinals for Joe Ferguson, because we

Tal Smith, president of baseball operations in Houston.
Courtesy of the Houston Astros.

needed a catcher. In those days, I didn't have to pick up the phone to talk with anyone else. That's how deals were made. GMs had much more communication than today. Now a lot of information is shared through emails and cell phones. It's not nearly as personal as it was."

While the changes in the game have certainly resulted in parity and excitement, they have also left many executives realizing the stark differences. In the old days, trades were made for different reasons than they are today.

"When I started following the game, teams felt that players acquired would help more than the others that they traded," said Fred Claire, the former general manager of the Los Angeles Dodgers, who spent three decades in that organization. "It's seldom that trades are made that way now. The structure of the game has changed so much.

"In those days, the great Dodger teams would have never thought of trading Roy Campanella, or Pee Wee Reese. If you go back to the late '40s, when I started following the game, I remember a trade that saw the Reds trade Hank Sauer [with Frank Baumholtz] to the Cubs for Harry Walker and Peanuts Lowrey. The team felt that the players acquired would help more than the others.

"You are making a deal to attempt to improve your team. It takes a tremendous amount of communication within your organization. You want to call upon the people who know your players, like scouts and player development people. They are important to the process because there is also a lot of research done about the player you are acquiring.

"Scouts are privy to a lot of background as far as what was behind the trade. They are often called on to give evaluations of players."

Different organizations have different organizational layouts and responsibilities. Pat Gillick is a veteran general manager with experience in Seattle, Toronto, Baltimore, and most recently, Philadelphia. He has his own system and structure in his organization that is geared toward making communication with other ball clubs an easy and regular process. That can only lead to worthwhile discussions that in turn can lead to trades that improve the team.

"Trades are made because people want to fill voids in their

Pat Gillick is a veteran GM who has built winning teams.
Courtesy of the Philadelphia Phillies.

clubs, or they have an excess on their club that they can use to strengthen their club in another area," he said. "The other thing is that trades are also made when the management of a team becomes discontented with the personality of a player on their club. A player could be considered a bad influence. So some trades are also personality trades.

"Since free agency and the increase of player compensation over the past thirty years, economics is an element that has come into the exchange of players. Before that you made a lot of good old baseball trades. You made a trade without much concern about economics on either side of the deal. I do miss that because it was much easier to trade for what you needed. You did not have to take into consideration the economic part.

"When I got in the business, there were a little more than half the teams we have now. We have our own situation here [in Philadelphia]. I have five of us who are assigned a certain number of clubs. Ruben Amaro Jr., Mike Arbuckle, Gordon Lakey, Charlie Kerfeld, and myself are all assigned a number of clubs, between five and seven. It's our job to stay in regular contact with those clubs and get an indication of feeling of what players could be available and what players we might have available. So rather than having one guy talking to thirty clubs, we split it up and the five of us talk every ten days on a conference call. Then I put things together. We're sort of like sales people. We have a certain number of clubs we have to stay in contact with and find out what their needs and excesses might be.

"I have the Mets, Yankees, Boston, and Atlanta. The other guys have six clubs apiece. It's a lot easier for me and it takes a little while to establish their authority. But once they get that established, the clubs know they have authority to speak for the Phillies. The more they talk and the more they make contact, it makes things a lot easier."

Sharing the workload is something that makes keeping up with other clubs a less challenging task. In the days where there were eight teams in each league, keeping in touch and up to date with other teams was not nearly as daunting a task.

"When I came back to the Astros at the end of the 1994 season, I was asked by Drayton McLane, the owner, to pare the payroll," said Tal Smith. "Ken Caminiti's contract was about to end and we tried to extend him to avoid his becoming a free agent. We were unable to do so and as a result we tried to make a trade to preserve some asset value. So we took all of the other clubs and divided them up between a number of us and made a study of the other clubs and tried to find out who might be interested in him and who might be expendable. So we had specialists on different organizations who gave you a thumbnail sketch about who might be available."

The result of their internal efforts was a successful trade, finalized on December 29, 1994, that saw the Astros send Caminiti, a player to be named later (Sean Fesh), Andujar Cedeno, Steve Finley, Roberto Petagine, and Brian Williams to the San Diego Padres in exchange for Derek Bell, Doug Brocail, Ricky Gutierrez, Pedro Martinez, Phil Plantier, and Craig Shipley. Caminiti earned $4.6 million for the Padres.

"It was much easier to make trades in those days," said Smith. "A lot of GMs don't even bother with the hospitality suites at the All-Star Game and World Series anymore. It used to be that they were comprised of general managers and key staff. Now there are hundreds of sponsors there. A lot of GMs don't even attend anymore. So we just send email messages."

Scouting plays a vitally important part in baseball. Facts, figures, and computer readouts are all part of the process, but in sports in general and baseball in particular, the human touch still plays an important role. Not only do scouts file reports on a team's upcoming opponents, but a big part of their job is evaluating and reporting on players around the major leagues, minor leagues, and of course, amateur leagues. Their opinions are valued and requested on a regular basis.

"When I was acting as GM, I had our scouts give a grade to every player in Major League Baseball with 10 being the best," said Bill Giles, chairman of the Philadelphia Phillies, who has spent his entire life in the game. "So if you need a left-handed-hitting outfielder, you could just go to the scouting reports and see who graded out well.

"When I traded for John Denny in 1982, I had Ray Shore as a scout from Cincinnati, who I felt was a great judge of pitching talent. The Cleveland Indians had John, who wasn't having a particularly good year. Another one of our scouts, Hugh Alexander, found out that the Indians were going to trade him in the wintertime. It was September and my wife and I were vacationing in Williamsburg, Virginia, with some other friends. I had called Gabe Paul, the GM of Cleveland, before I left on vacation and asked if he might trade Denny. He said he might, so while we were away on vacation I was on the phone for two or three days trying to make the trade, which we ultimately did. My wife was so furious with me we almost got a divorce."

On September 12 of that year, Giles acquired John Denny from Cleveland in exchange for Wil Culmer, Jerry Reed, and Roy Smith. The following season, Denny won nineteen games and helped the Phillies get to the World Series against the Baltimore Orioles. Bill and Nancy Giles remain a happily married couple.

"A lot of trades used to happen at the winter meetings," Giles said. "Each club would have a suite at the hotel. The scouts and the manager would go to the lobby and ask about a particular player and if the team would be willing to trade the player. If they said yes, a meeting would be held in the suite.

"When Paul Owens was our GM, his style of trading was to ask for a player that he knew he had no chance to get, but still offer something in exchange. Then, he'd settle for something less: the player he wanted all along."

While general managers had the ability to wheel and deal on

Paul Owens was a legendary trader.
Courtesy of the Philadelphia Phillies.

their own in the old days of the game, even then most trades were
the result of a combination of factors that would include a need,
an overabundance in a particular area, and regular discussions with
scouts who work for the organization. Scouts are the eyes and ears
of a team; they put life into the plethora of statistics that baseball
is inundated with.

Good, dependable scouts are worth their weight in gold, as they
have the ability to research not just what stats a player can put up

but also that player as a person and teammate. That due diligence can make trades successful without necessarily showing up in the box score.

"We do our job," wrote Atlanta Braves general manager John Schuerholz in his book, *Built to Win*. "In order to win 14 consecutive division championships and five National League championships and a World Series, you have to do all the facets of your work well. You have to analyze your scouting reports. You have to listen to scouts. You have to hear what they say and see their expressions. You have to hear them pitch a player and know the ability of the scout. Of course, you also have to have a basis of reliability on a player's productivity—statistics.

"Every player I've ever traded for or every acquisition I've made to this day, I would have somebody in our organization prepare a dossier that included all the scouting reports and all the statistics for his entire career. Day games, night games, artificial turf, grass, home games, road games, before the All-Star Game, after the All-Star Game, against right-handers, against left-handers, against amphibious mammals. Tom Ferrick [former major league player and scout] was right: Stats don't lie. But they also don't tell the complete story."

Schuerholz has steered the ship during the Braves' climb to dominance in the National League. The talent that has appeared on the playing field for a decade and a half only mirrors the all-stars that Atlanta has in its front office. According to Schuerholz, his scouting staff ranks right at the top of his list of important members of the organization. Of course, it also helps to give their opinions serious consideration before either making a trade or deciding to pass.

Schuerholz explained, "We're going to use the judgment and the intuition and the knowledge and gut feel of the Paul Snyders and Jim Fregosis and Chuck McMichaels and the Frank Wrens and the Dean Taylors. And the Chuck LaMars and Dayton Moores and Roy Clarks and Tyrone Brookses. Our scouts and executives.

"I'm going to use their passion about a player. When Roy Clark, our scouting director, stands up in a group discussion about a potential trade and says with emphasis that he would not trade a certain minor league player because of this and this and this, I admire that conviction, that passion. I think that's healthy. And Roy typically will add: 'Obviously, John, whatever decision you make we're behind you. But I want you to know how I feel about this guy.'

(Actually, Roy likes to playfully say, 'We're with you, boss, win or tie.')

"Because I rely so heavily upon the input from our scouting and player development staffs before I reach a final decision on most any roster move, I put just as much emphasis and care in the formation of that staff roster as I do our player roster.

"Scouts are, in a manner of speaking, like major league players. You bring players to your team because you think they have the ability to strengthen the team you're assembling. And it's no different with the scouting team. You make presumptions based on a guy's past record, based on his reputation in the industry, based on your personal knowledge of him, based on recommendations from people you trust. Just like you put together your baseball team, you put together your scouting team."

At the apex of the Major League Baseball team is when the various elements of the organization are all on the same page and a major trade is completed. On June 15, 1977, one of the most memorable deals in the history of the game saw the New York Mets trade their future Hall of Fame right-handed pitching ace Tom Seaver to the Cincinnati Reds in exchange for Pat Zachry, Doug Flynn, Steve Henderson, and Dan Norman. While that deal garnered most of the national headlines, as is always the case, other teams were also involved in improving their ball clubs via the trade.

This example of a trade gives a front-row seat to just some of the trials and tribulations involved in making a trade even before the rigors of impending free agency.

As fate would have it, veteran baseball writer Bill Conlin was in Cincinnati that night covering the series between the visiting Phillies and the hometown Reds. While the press box was abuzz with news about the Seaver trade, Philadelphia general manager Paul "Pope" Owens gave his friend Conlin a worthwhile tip: Don't leave with the rest of the press corps after the game. Something was up.

"The Seaver trade was announced during the game," Conlin said. "The only people left in the press box were one or two Philadelphia writers who were on deadline. That was a huge story and was one of the most widely covered trades of all time. Seaver was considered the best pitcher in the National League.

"Paul Owens stopped by my seat in the press box and asked me how I was getting home to Philadelphia after the game. I told him I was planning on being on the team's charter flight and he suggested that I shouldn't do that. He and top scout Hugh Alexander were staying behind and that the trade deadline was midnight that night. I knew something big was up and Pope even got the hotel room I checked out of before the game back for me.

"The Pope's suite was right down the hall from mine and they were on the phone constantly. The Phillies' brass had agreed in principle that day to a trade that in my mind cemented not only the division title that year, but for several years to come. They agreed to acquire outfielder Bake McBride from the St. Louis Cardinals in exchange for pitcher Tom Underwood and outfielders Dane Iorg and Rick Bosetti. The holdup was that McBride had bad knees and the Phillies wanted to talk to the Cardinals' team doctor, Dr. Stan London, before signing off on the deal. The problem was that Dr. London was on vacation in Las Vegas. They had people calling casino after casino paging Dr. Stan London, leaving messages all over the city to call urgently.

"The other problem they had that night was that Dallas Green, who had been in charge of the farm system, was viciously and violently opposed to the trade because Underwood was one of his prized draft picks and he was almost as high on Iorg and Bosetti. He told Hughie Alexander he'd resign if they made the deal. He got over it, but they had to placate Green between calls to Las Vegas.

"They finally got in contact with the doctor and the deal was finalized at 2:16 a.m. As luck would have it, I had a 5 a.m. deadline for the paper so I had a tremendous exclusive on the damn thing. I flew back to the city the next day and my story was the lead story on our paper."

But as the years have passed, the art of trading has changed. Gone are the days of the smoke-filled gin mill, where stories and players were swapped with the regularity of another round of drinks.

"That is just part of the evolution of the game," said Fred Claire. "The role of the general manager and the structure of the process itself are much more sophisticated. The days of trades made at the bar are gone. Throughout the '70s, the game was changed dramatically. And teams have changed in a like manner. I think that we in baseball and in life really have to deal with what is."

Picking some of the biggest and most interesting trades in the history of the game is a daunting task, but sometimes the pure name recognition does the trick. Some were blockbusters and some were highway robbery, while others really helped both teams. One thing that all of these trades have in common is that they were made in a calmer, simpler time when players were exchanged to help the team play better. And there were also examples of players who had simply worn out their welcome at a specific locale.

FRANKIE FRISCH FOR ROGERS HORNSBY

Six years after the deal that saw Babe Ruth sold to the New York Yankees, the New York Giants dealt Frankie Frisch and Jimmy

Ring to the St. Louis Cardinals in exchange for Rogers Hornsby on December 20, 1926, in what has to be considered the first actual blockbuster trade. This deal could definitely be seen as a personality trade.

This trade was not what the St. Louis faithful expected to happen to their player-manager, who had won his first Most Valuable Player award in 1925 en route to leading the Cardinals to the World Series title. It was as if Hornsby could not be valuable enough to owner Sam Breadon. While the star second baseman was the embodiment of all things great on the baseball field, he reportedly had a belligerent and icy relationship with management.

The final straw occurred during a contract dispute in which Hornsby insisted on a three-year contract, while Breadon would commit to just one. While Hornsby lasted just one season in New York, he put up outstanding numbers. Back in St. Louis, Frankie Frisch and Jimmy Ring had lots to prove.

Frankie Frisch had his own problems with management in general and John McGraw in particular. He had been instrumental in four consecutive pennants for the Giants, but the time for a change was apparent. He was more than able to accept the challenge in St. Louis. In his first season in St. Louis, he finished second in MVP voting, hitting .337. He also had 641 assists and 1,059 chances at second base. He would spend ten more seasons with the Cardinals, playing on four more pennant-winning teams.

Coming off an 11-10 season with the Giants, Ring had a nondescript 0-4 campaign with the Cardinals in 1927 before being traded to the Phillies the following winter, along with catcher Johnny Schulte, in exchange for catcher Bubber Jonnard, shortstop Jimmy Cooney, and outfielder Johnny Mokan. Ring completed his 118-149 twelve-year career in 1928 with Philadelphia amassing a 4-17 record.

This blockbuster of a deal saw a pair of future Hall of Famers change address after circumstances had made it virtually impossi-

Frankie Frisch (left) and Rogers Hornsby (right): a blockbuster of a trade.
National Baseball Hall of Fame Library, Cooperstown, NY.

ble for them to remain with their original clubs. So a deal was made that both clubs felt comfortable with.

After a solid year in New York in which he hit .361, Hornsby was on the move once again, as he had had problems with manager John McGraw. He was sent to the Boston Braves in exchange for Shanty Hogan and Jimmy Welsh. Hornsby responded with a great year statistically in which he won his final batting title, hitting .387, and was also named manager of the club. But he was then sent packing to the Chicago Cubs in a deal for Socks Seibold, Percy Jones, Lou Legett, Freddie Maguire, Bruce Cunningham, and $200,000. The 1929 season was a good one for Hornsby as he hit .380, but then he began to slow down.

Conversely, Frankie Frisch found a home in St. Louis following the trade from New York. He spent the final eleven years of his playing career and began his illustrious managerial career there as well.

HANK SAUER AND FRANKIE BAUMHOLTZ FOR PEANUTS AND THE HAT

Sometimes an older player is actually more like a fine wine, getting better with age. Other times an aging player is just a ballplayer who is getting old and past his prime. The thing that teams need to do is to distinguish between those possibilities. For Cincinnati Reds fans, unfortunately, the organization blew it in 1949 when deciding on the future of thirty-two-year-old left fielder Hank Sauer.

The popular power-hitting outfielder had a breakout season with the Reds in 1948, hitting .260 while smacking thirty-five home runs and driving in ninety-seven runs. But the Cincinnati front office saw an aging, slow player who was off to a slumping start in 1949, struggling with a .237 average with just four homers after forty-two games. So, considering him a one-season wonder, the Reds sent Sauer and another outfielder, Frankie Baumholtz, to the Chicago Cubs in exchange for outfielders Harry "Peanuts" Lowrey and Harry "The Hat" Walker. While the Reds got two players with colorful nicknames, Chicago got a certified home run threat in Hank Sauer.

Following the trade, Sauer hit .291 in Chicago with twenty-seven home runs and 93 RBIs during the balance of the '49 season. In his first full season with the Cubs, Sauer blossomed into a consistent source of power in the lineup with thirty-seven homers and 103 RBIs while hitting a very respectable .274. After having another solid year in 1951, the '52 campaign was an outstanding one that saw him garner national attention, as well as the adoration of the Cubs faithful. Sauer hit .270, leading the National League in homers with thirty-seven and RBIs with 121, earning the Most Valuable Player award. His last huge season came in 1954 when he hit a career-high forty-one homers, adding 103 RBIs with a .288 batting average.

During his career, Sauer hit three home runs in a game twice, in 1950 and '52. Ironically, both times he did the hat trick against Phillies southpaw hurler Curt Simmons.

While Baumholtz struggled early on with Chicago, he soon regained the form he displayed during his first two seasons in Cincinnati, when he hit .283 and .296. In five full seasons with the Cubs, he had solid seasons hitting .284, .325 (which was second best in the league in 1952), .306, .297, and .289. Baumholtz was also a two-sport star, earning an All-Star berth when he averaged fourteen points per game with the Cleveland Rebels, of the National Basketball Association. But his first, full-time love was baseball.

While the deal worked out well in Chicago, it was one that most Reds fans would like to forget. While Sauer and Baumholtz aged like fine wine in Chicago, the combination of Lowrey and Walker had a nasty vinegar taste in Cincinnati.

Harry "The Hat" Walker had a long career in baseball. He is

The Harry "Peanuts" Lowrey (left) and Hank Sauer (right) trade caused sadness in Cincy. National Baseball Hall of Fame Library, Cooperstown, NY.

probably best known for his double in the seventh game of the 1946 World Series that drove in his Cardinals teammate Enos Slaughter with the run that captured the Fall Classic title for St. Louis over the Boston Red Sox. Walker won the batting title for the Phillies with a .363 average in 1947, but when he held out in a salary dispute the following spring, a roster spot was earned by future Hall of Fame center fielder Richie Ashburn. Even though he eventually signed in time to play in 112 games for the Phillies with a respectable .292 average, he was traded to Chicago after the season in exchange for Bill Nicholson.

Prior to the trade from Chicago to Cincinnati, Walker was hitting .264, and he hit .318 for the Reds following the trade. But after the season ended, the Reds traded him back to St. Louis for Lou Klein and Ron Northey, whom he had been traded for once before.

In addition to being a serviceable outfielder for thirteen big-league seasons with a .273 lifetime batting average, "Peanuts" Lowrey was also an actor who appeared in numerous movies during his playing career, including *Pride of the Yankees* in 1942, *The Stratton Story* in 1949, and *The Winning Team* in 1952. His act on the playing field was also quite good, as this hitter never hit below .257 with Chicago and had his best year in 1948 when he hit a career-high .294. He was batting at a .270 clip with the Cubs when the deal was made and hit .275 for the Reds.

The following year, Lowrey got off to a brutal start in Cincinnati, hitting just .227 in ninety-one games before he was purchased by St. Louis. With the Cardinals, he returned to his former self, hitting .303 in 1951. He had a couple more productive big-league campaigns before ending his playing career in 1955 at the age of thirty-seven.

In what was certainly a case of mistaken identity, the Reds felt that Hank Sauer was an old player well past his prime. Little did they realize that he was just entering into his prime when they traded him.

ROCKY COLAVITO FOR HARVEY KUENN

In Boston there was the Curse of the Bambino. But in Cleveland, there is the Curse of Rocky Colavito. Since the Easter Sunday trade of Colavito to the Detroit Tigers in exchange for Harvey Kuenn, baseball in Cleveland has not been a box of chocolates. In fact, the city's fans are some of the most loyal and suffering in America's Game.

In what has to be considered a blockbuster of a deal, the Cleveland Indians dealt the popular Rocky Colavito, the reigning home run co-champion, to the Detroit Tigers for the reigning batting champion, Harvey Kuenn, on Easter Sunday, April 17, 1960. Colavito was a fan favorite in Cleveland, a handsome, friendly slugger who never turned down a fan who wanted an autograph in his life. While the trade worked out well for Detroit, it was a disaster in Cleveland.

The year before the deal was struck, Colavito hit .257 for the second-place Indians with forty-two homers and 111 RBIs. The previous season, he hit .303 with forty-one dingers and 113 RBIs. In his final year with the fourth-place Tigers, Kuenn won the batting title with a .353 average, but he hit just nine homers, driving in seventy-one runs.

The trade was met with utter disdain in Cleveland. The fans were in an uproar over the departure of their favorite player. Frank Lane, the general manager who engineered the deal, had a favorite saying that pretty much summed up his personality and his interest in the unhappiness of the loyals. "Sympathy," Lane would say, "you can find that in the dictionary, right between shit and syphilis." That was a saying he would often quote when hearing about other people's challenges in life.

A native of the Bronx, Rocky Colavito was a fan of the Yankees in general and Joe DiMaggio in particular. He was signed by the Indians in 1950. He worked his way through the Cleveland system until he had his first taste of major league action in 1955. After starting out the following season in Triple A, Colavito rejoined the Tribe in July and hit .276 while belting twenty-one home runs. He progressed until 1958 and 1959, when his home run totals made him the darling of the city by the lake. Only adding to his popularity was his strong throwing arm, which he gladly showed off at every opportunity.

There are those who feel that Rocky Colavito became the stuff of legend in Cleveland on the night of June 10, 1959. The slugger had been mired in a hitting slump and there was a newspaper report that he was about to be traded to the Boston Red Sox in exchange for Jackie Jensen.

Colavito walked in his first at bat. The second time up against Jerry Walker in the third inning, he lined a homer into the left-field bleachers. Then in the fifth and sixth innings, he hit two more dingers against Arnold Portocarrero. Up until this game, no single player had ever hit more than two home runs in Baltimore. Pitcher Ernie Johnson had not allowed a home run all season. But Colavito nailed a fast ball over the fence in left field to complete his four-homer onslaught.

As spring training loomed in the future, Frank Lane and Rocky Colavito began yet another bitter contract exchange. Colavito made $28,000 in 1959 and had a phenomenal year and asked for $45,000 in 1960. As spring training began, he was holding out. But a trade rumor about the Colavito-for-Kuenn deal once again surfaced. Colavito signed for $35,000, a $7,000 range.

Harvey Kuenn was signed by the Tigers in 1952 and became the starting shortstop later that season. In his first full big-league season, the line drive hitter had a .308 season in which he led the majors with 209 hits, setting a major league rookie mark with 167 singles. He continued to hit for average, but was switched to the outfield because of questionable range on the field.

After leading the league in hitting, Kuenn asked for $50,000 in 1960. He then lowered his demand to $47,000, but finally accepted Tigers general manager Bill DeWitt's offer of $42,000 after the trade rumors spread. Like Colavito, Kuenn got just a $7,000 raise after what was a great season.

Then the deal was struck, even though Frank Lane told Colavito that he would not trade him to Detroit for Kuenn.

"We were playing an exhibition game in Memphis," Colavito told Terry Pluto in his book, *The Curse of Rocky Colavito.* "It was our last spring game before the regular season opened. We were playing the White Sox, and in my first at bat, I hit a home run to left field. In my next at bat, I was at first base after a force play. Joe Gordon [Cleveland's manager] came out to me and said, 'That is the last time you'll bat in a Cleveland uniform.' I looked at him, not really wanting to hear what he was going to tell me. Gordon said, 'You've been traded to Detroit for Harvey Kuenn.'

"There I was, still standing on first base, and this guy is telling me that I'm traded. Then Gordon said, 'I want to wish you all the luck in the world.' All I could think to say was, 'The same to you.' But Gordon spread the story that I said, 'Kuenn and who else?' That was the biggest lie ever. It implied that I didn't think Harvey was good enough to be traded for me. That wasn't it at all. I just couldn't believe they did it. It caught me totally by surprise. But I never said anything negative about Harvey Kuenn. After that, I never had any stomach for Gordon or Lane."

A local writer, Gordon Cobbledick, wrote about Cleveland's departed favorite son in the *Cleveland Plain Dealer.* "No more than a half dozen players in the history of Cleveland baseball have been accorded the hero worship he enjoys. Rocky was our boy. We raised him. He first came to our attention as a 17-year-old who won the Class D Florida State League home run championship at Daytona in 1951. We followed his career through a disappointing season at Spartanburg, and another home run title at Reading and still another at Indianapolis, knowing that someday he would be hitting them for the Indians. We saw him, finally, and almost at once, took him to our hearts."

And then he was gone.

Without their marquee strong-armed, power-hitting outfielder, the Indians finished in fourth place in 1960 with a 76-78 record. Kuenn struggled with injuries and hit .308 with nine homers and fifty-four RBIs. Following the season, he was traded to the San Francisco Giants in exchange for pitcher Johnny Antonelli, who went 0-4 in eleven games, and outfielder Willie Kirkland, who had three mediocre seasons for the Tribe. Colavito had four strong seasons in Detroit, hitting 35, 45, 37, and 22 home runs.

The deal was such a disappointment in Cleveland that it was thought to result in the Curse of Rocky Colavito for the Indians. The Tribe had won the World Series in 1948, but never came within eleven games of first place after the trade was made until they won the American League pennant in 1997.

And lost the World Series.

BROCK FOR BROGLIO?

Remember Bing Devine's fourth simple rule? You've got to get lucky.

Devine also followed the other rules that include needing the player, listening to talent evaluators, and having the guts to make the deal. But in the history of America's Game, there are countless examples of potential that never reaches fruition. And every now and then, you catch lightning in a jar.

During the early stages of the 1964 season, the St. Louis Cardinals had a strong team that consisted of a multitude of fine players. But as the season progressed and the Philadelphia Phillies had a comfortable lead in the standings, Devine and manager Johnny Keane came to the conclusion that something was missing. The Cards were without Stan "The Man" Musial, who had retired at the conclusion of the 1963 campaign, and left fielder Charlie James wasn't setting the world on fire.

Two young pitchers, Bob Gibson and Ray Sadecki, were pitching well and adding some depth to the pitching rotation. It enabled the team to part with a veteran pitcher for an outfielder who might just have the missing ingredient that was needed in St. Louis.

On June 15, 1964, one of the most one-sided trades in the history of the game occurred when Devine and the St. Louis Cardinals acquired future Hall of Fame outfielder and base-stealing champion Lou Brock, along with pitchers Jack Spring and Paul Toth, from the Chicago Cubs in exchange for pitchers Ernie Broglio and Bobby Shantz and outfielder Doug Clemens.

"We had indicated our interest in Brock to the Cubs for a long time," Devine wrote in his book, *The Memoirs of Bing Devine*. "But John Holland, the Cubs' general manager, always rejected it. He'd say, 'We're not going to deal him.'

"But when we were in Los Angeles the day before the deadline, I was making the rounds by phone from Dodger Stadium, calling other general managers to see if we could do anything to improve the Cardinals. And when I called John Holland this time, he said, 'If you're still interested, we might have to move Brock.'

"I said, 'For what?'

"He said, 'We need a pitcher. You gave me a list of players when we talked before and we'll take a pitcher off that list. We'll take Broglio.'

"Ernie Broglio was one of our top starting pitchers. He had won 18 games the year before. I told Holland, 'I'll have to check with our manager.'

"Our manager was Johnny Keane. I told Johnny we had a chance to get Brock for Broglio, and he said, 'What are we waiting for?'

"Most of the fans and media in St. Louis didn't think much of Brock for Broglio. Broglio had won 20 games for us in 1960 before winning those 18 games in '63. But in '64, he was 3-5 for us in 11 games when we made the trade.

"Brock had been a regular for the Cubs for two years. He hit .263 in '62 and .258 in '63 and he stole only 16 bases the first year, when Maury Wills led the league with 104, and just 24 the next year."

So the deal was struck and history was made. Spring and Toth, the two throw-ins from the Cubs, did little in St. Louis, while Shantz and Clemens did even less in Chicago than Broglio did. And while Broglio insists he did not suffer an arm injury until after the trade was made, that was where Bing Devine and the St. Louis Cardinals got lucky.

"Broglio had some success with us in St. Louis," said his former teammate, Doug Clemens. "He had a big, breaking curveball and a good fastball. He was quite a competitor. There was some thought that his arm might have been hurt before the trade was made, but that's never been proven."

Making a trade to help your team is one thing. But most general managers would absolutely not send damaged goods to another team. Although Broglio's arm problems began shortly after the trade, Bing Devine was a well-respected baseball man who would not be thought of as the type who would knowingly trade an injured player to a different team. The stakes are just too high at that level.

"The word of the general manager about the health of the players is the most essential part of any deal," said Fred Claire. "It is your credibility and your word that is on the line. Good deals are deals that work and work for both clubs. As a GM, your credibility is so important because you need the trust of the other teams."

The Brock-for-Broglio deal goes down in the history of the game as one of the most one-sided deals of all time. Short-term, the Cardinals won the National League pennant in 1964, and long-term, Lou Brock became a member of the Baseball Hall of Fame.

FERGUSON JENKINS FOR LARRY JACKSON AND BOB BUHL

While the Chicago Cubs certainly got the worst of the Brock-for-Broglio trade, that's not to say that the organization hasn't made

Fred Claire, former Los Angeles Dodgers GM.
Courtesy of the Los Angeles Dodgers.

some stunningly successful deals as well. Two such deals came at the expense of the Philadelphia Phillies.

After blowing the National League pennant in 1964, Philadelphia felt much pressure to bring home the gold in 1965. In retrospect, the '64 team that led the National League until its fabled collapse in the final two weeks was more than likely a team that overachieved. To expect the same kind of magic the following season was not realistic. The team foundered and by the spring of 1966, it became obvious that the Phillies would need to make some big changes to try to recapture the magic of 1964. It was felt that veteran pitching was needed to complete a rotation starting with Jim Bunning and Chris Short.

Blessed with a solid minor league system, the Phillies had some fine young prospects that had honed their skills in their farm system and had had good success on their Little Rock Triple A team, which won a championship in 1963. One of those players was right-handed pitcher Ferguson Jenkins. While Jenkins experienced some success at the minor league level, he was thought of by the Phillies brass as a control pitcher who was not blessed with the stuff to be a big winner on the major league level.

In the Windy City, the Chicago Cubs were having a difficult time getting out of the second division and manager Leo Durocher had reportedly broached the subject of replacing aging first baseman Ernie Banks. Chicago tried to acquire powerful Orlando Cepeda from San Francisco, offering former twenty-game winner Dick Ellsworth. But the Giants preferred a deal which brought them another talented southpaw pitcher, Ray Sadecki. Two teams in need of a jolt of positive energy got together to improve their clubs with the best of intentions. The result was one of the most lopsided trades in the history of baseball.

Veteran Cubs right-handers Larry Jackson and Bob Buhl each had enjoyed many successful big-league campaigns and the Phillies' brass felt they both had enough fuel left in the tank to get them over the top and back into contention. A deal was struck on April 21, 1966, which brought those two hurlers to Philadelphia in exchange for first baseman/outfielder John Herrnstein, outfielder Adolpho Phillips, and of course, Ferguson Jenkins.

"Phillies manager Gene Mauch thought that Jackson was a solid third starter behind Jim Bunning and Chris Short, and he was," said writer Bill Conlin. "Mauch also thought that Buhl would be a solid fourth starter, but he was done.

"Mauch didn't think that Jenkins threw hard enough to be an effective starter. He thought the ultimate career destination for

Fergie was middle relief. He thought he could throw a double play ball with his sinker. He was just a young guy at the time. Mauch did not have a good touch with pitchers and young players. They were his tragic flaws. He was the guy who once said that he felt that Robin Roberts was pitching like Dolly Madison.

"When Jenkins was traded to Chicago, Roberts was there and claims that he insisted that the Cubs get Fergie in the deal. The Phillies never had Jenkins long enough to find out he was a tremendous competitor with a rubber arm who could throw strikes at the knees on command. That streak of six consecutive twenty-win seasons at Wrigley Field was in my opinion one of the greatest pitching feats of all time."

Jackson went 41-45 in three years with the Phillies and Buhl went 6-8 in 1966 and was released after just three appearances the following year. The Cubs had sought after Herrnstein, who hit .234 while getting significant playing time with the '64 Phillies. But the former University of Michigan football captain was never able to replicate the big numbers he put up in Triple A in 1962 and '63, when he hit twenty-three and twenty-two home runs, respectively. After just nine games in Chicago, he was sent to Atlanta in exchange for Marty Keough and Arnold Early and soon disappeared.

The fleet Phillips played well in the Cubs outfield, combining power with speed. In 1966 he hit a respectable .262, slugging sixteen home runs with thirty-six RBIs and thirty-two stolen bases. He had his best big-league campaign the following year when he hit .268, with seventeen homers, seventy RBIs and twenty-four steals. But his productivity trailed off and he was dealt to Montreal in June of 1969. But the jewel of the deal for the Cubbies was Ferguson Jenkins.

Used as a spot starter and reliever for the balance of the 1966 season, he responded with a 6-8 record in what would be a career-high sixty-one games. But the decision was made to give him the ball every four days in the starting rotation beginning in 1967, and the lanky native from Ontario won 20, 20, 21, 22, 24, and 20 games in consecutive seasons. He struggled with a 14-16 record with the Cubs in 1973, was dealt to Texas, and responded with a 25-12 record for the Rangers in 1974.

The Hall of Fame pitcher won 284 big-league games, all but two following his trade from Philadelphia.

Big trades continued to be orchestrated by major league general managers, but the die was being cast in two cities that would have a dramatic effect on the future of Major League Baseball. For decades, in baseball, a trade was made to fill a need, rid an organization of a troublesome player, strengthen the team by dealing an excess for a need, or simply help the bottom line by conducting a fire sale. But because of some discontent in Philadelphia and St. Louis, baseball was about to change completely, with the owners losing the iron-fisted control they had had over the players for generations.

RICHIE ALLEN FOR CURT FLOOD

As the years progressed, there were no more serious challenges to baseball's reserve clause and little changed. Player holdouts became prevalent, as they used the only real leverage they had in salary disputes with management. But as players continued to be sent packing with no say whatsoever, circumstances were underway that would lead to the most serious challenge ever to the power of baseball. While Curt Flood was certainly the point man in the battle to come, the real springboard of the controversy was none other than a power-hitting first baseman from Wampum, Pennsylvania, named Richie Allen.

Allen was a powerful player with seemingly unlimited ability when he first made the Phillies' team in 1964, the year in which he would subsequently be named the National League Rookie of the Year after hitting .318 with twenty-nine homers and ninety-one RBIs. He also led the league in runs with 125 and triples with thirteen. But he also led the league with forty-one errors at third base, a position he was switched to from the outfield in spring training.

Fresh off of what was considered one of the worst collapses in baseball history, the 1965 edition of the Philadelphia Phillies enjoyed none of the magic of the previous year's team, which played way over its head for much of the season. This team struggled to play .500 baseball. But a fan favorite was veteran slugger Frank Thomas, who injected some needed energy and offense into the '64 Phillies, hitting .294 with seven home runs and twenty-six RBIs in thirty-nine games before breaking his thumb, which skipper Gene Mauch was known to have said was the major factor that caused the epic swoon of the club.

Frustrated by Mauch's constant platooning and reportedly at odds with some of the black players on the team, Thomas was hitting a light .260 when fireworks went off a day early, on July 3. Some of Thomas's antics had already riled up other members of the team.

"There was one thing that Frank Thomas used to do that I could never get out of my mind," Dick Allen wrote in his book, *Crash: The Life and Times of Dick Allen*, with Tim Whitaker. "He would pretend to offer his hand in a soul shake to a young player on the team, but when the player would offer his hand in return, Thomas would grab the player's thumb and bend it back hard. To Thomas, it was a big joke. But I saw too many brothers on the team with swollen thumbs to get any laughs.

"I was down third base fielding ground balls. Thomas was in the cage taking batting practice. Johnny Callison stopped by third base. He had a big grin on his face. He said, 'Let's fuck with Lurch.'

"But instead of answering Callison's taunts, Thomas glares down the third-base line at me and screams, 'What are you trying to be, another Muhammad Clay, always running your mouth off?'

Dick Allen was part of a trade that revolutionized the game.
Courtesy of the Philadelphia Phillies.

Thomas knew it was Callison who had taunted him. The Muhammad Clay remark was meant to say a lot and it reminded me of how he would bend back a black player's thumb for laughs.

"I went over, right in his face. I said, 'Frank, I told you, that stuff don't go with me.' Then I popped him, a short left to the jaw. He went down, then he got up swinging that bat. I ducked, but he caught me on the left shoulder. I just wanted to teach him a lesson. Now I wanted to kill."

During the July 3 ball game, Allen had a pair of hits and Thomas hit a pinch hit home run, his first of the season. But after the contest, a 10-8 loss to the Cincinnati Reds, the Phillies parted ways with Thomas, putting him on irrevocable waivers. Mauch enforced a gag rule on the team, threatening fines if any of them spoke with the press about the incident. In fact, Allen would have been fined $2,000 if he had spoken about what happened.

As a result, a popular player was released and a young, budding star was blamed by the fans and the media. It was the beginning of the end for Richie Allen in Philadelphia. Although it would still be another five years until he was traded, the problems began with the Frank Thomas incident. That situation got worse as the years progressed, with a litany of examples of the slugger and the organization constantly at odds. Missed games, heavy drinking, suspensions, and mysterious injuries were the norm as Richie Allen continued to show great talent on the baseball field and what was thought of as unstable behavior off the field.

In one of the great ironies, Allen was not a malcontent at all, by today's standards, just an individual with tons of talent who needed a little added attention. But the situation grew progressively worse and worse until it was certain that at the conclusion of the 1969 season Richie Allen would be gone.

In St. Louis, the Cardinals were a team blessed with All-Star-caliber players that included Bill White, Tim McCarver, Bob Gibson, Dick Groat, Ken Boyer, and center fielder Curt Flood.

Flood was an outstanding center fielder who ranked third in the history of the National League when he retired with 1,683 games in center, behind Willie Mays and Richie Ashburn. He led the league in putouts four times and in fielding percentage twice, and was awarded Gold Gloves from 1963 to 1969. While he had great natural ability, Flood's excellence defensively had as much to do with preparation as it did talent.

"The most difficult play for the center fielder is the ball hit right at him," wrote Tim McCarver in his book, *Baseball for Brain Surgeons and Other Fans*. "The fielder may have trouble breaking on it properly because he can't tell how far it is going. When Curt Flood played center field, he judged the distance by the bill of his cap. If the ball was above the bill, he broke back; if it was below the bill, he broke in. The lower the ball is hit, the quicker the fielder's reactions while going forward must be. Then it's very important for him to gauge how hard it was hit."

No slouch at the plate, Flood hit .300 or better six times and led the league in hits with 211 in 1964, his first year as an All-Star. To be sure, he was putting together a career that would have been considered at least that of a borderline potential Hall of Famer.

After helping St. Louis reach the World Series in consecutive seasons, hitting .335 in 1967 and .301 in 1968, Flood's average dipped to .285 in 1969 as the team slumped to fourth place in the National League, thirteen games behind the New York Mets. Even before the season began, during spring training in St. Petersburg, Cardinals owner Augie Busch, growing tired of player complaints about salaries, went on a public rant with reporters present.

Busch said, in part, "Fans are no longer as sure as they were before about their high regard for the game and the players. Too many fans are saying our players are getting fat, that they think only of money, and less about the game itself. And it's the game the fans love and have enjoyed and paid for all these years.

"The fans will be looking at you this year more critically than ever before to watch how you perform and see whether you really are giving everything you have. If we don't have the right attitudes, if we don't give everything we have to show those who pay their way into the park, then you can be sure they'll know it."

Flood took the attack to heart. His attitude may have suffered and he may have been looked upon as a troublemaker, whom the club would be better off without. But he and other players in the clubhouse felt that the comments by Busch set a negative tone for the season. Was it a self-fulfilling prophecy, or did the owner spot the need to shake things up before anyone else noticed? Regard-less, the comments he made did not sit well with the players.

"Mr. Busch destroyed the intangible this team had," Flood said, "its unity and its feeling of pride in being a part of the Cardinals organization. We never got over that."

After spending twelve seasons with the Cardinals, the thirty-one-year-old was packaged in a major trade. On October 7, 1969, Flood was sent to the Philadelphia Phillies along with McCarver, outfielder Byron Browne, and left-handed reliever Joe Hoerner in exchange for Allen, infielder Cookie Rojas, and right-handed pitcher Jerry Johnson.

"Why did I do that?" asked Cardinals then–general manager Bing Devine in his book. "To get Richie Allen. That part of the deal was controversial, too, because Allen had a reputation of being hard to handle.

"Flood never did report to the Phillies. He was protesting the reserve clause, which gave a team the right to control a player's movement once he was their property. That's what Flood objected to, being considered somebody's property with no chance to decide where he would work.

"When you think about it, the ball club had these players from the time they were signed in the minor leagues, to when they were brought up to the big leagues, for as long as the team wanted to keep them, to do whatever the team wanted with them. The players had no control over their careers.

"It's opposed to what the Constitution stands for—freedom. And I recognized that it was wrong. But I didn't know when I made that trade that I was opening the Flood gates."

Of course, hindsight is 20/20 and Devine's comments were made decades after the trade was made. At the time, both teams were happy with the deal and fans from both cities looked forward to a new season with their new charges. But then a funny thing happened. Curt Flood, a man of principle, refused to go to Philadelphia, which he labeled the "Northernmost Southern City." He apparently considered Philadelphia to be a racist city with belligerent fans, which was also saddled with a poor baseball team and a dilapidated Connie Mack Stadium

Flood learned of the trade on a radio broadcast he heard while driving his car. From his perspective, being traded was bad enough, but being dealt to Philadelphia was too much to contend with. He viewed the City of Brotherly Love as a racist town and also felt that much of the difficulty that Allen had to endure in Philadelphia was based on racism.

Flood refused to play for the Phillies, which basically ended his playing career at thirty-one years of age. In 1970, he filed a lawsuit against Major League Baseball over the reserve clause. He wanted the opportunity to choose what team he would play for and likened the plight of a player owned by a baseball club to being a slave one hundred years earlier.

While Flood was contemplating the much more serious implications of baseball's ability to trade players at will, in Philadelphia, there was genuine joy over the trade. Allen was gone and a number of outstanding players would be coming to the Phillies in exchange. Or so they thought.

"The whole thing was forced by Richie Allen just hammering, hammering, and hammering the Phillies organization to trade him until there was just no other direction to go," said Bill Conlin, a writer and columnist for the *Philadelphia Daily News* since 1965. "At one point Allen wasn't speaking to the Philadelphia media. But when the New York media came around the clubhouse he was very accommodating to them. They knew he was pushing to get traded and he told them in no uncertain terms that he'd love to play for the New York Mets. During the last road game that year in Shea Stadium, for the first time in his career, Allen hit three home runs. Each was longer than the other. The last hit the team bus way out beyond the fence in left field, where that apple is now. He hit the ball at least 450 feet trying to make a powerful statement as to what he could provide to the New York Mets.

"When he was finally traded to St. Louis, it was a helluva deal for the Phillies that was agreed on by Bing Devine and John Quinn [Phillies General Manager]. The Phillies got Flood, an All-Star-level center fielder, McCarver, a top-level catcher, Byron Browne, a very good fourth outfielder and a good guy in the clubhouse, and Joe Hoerner, a premier relief pitcher. It was a really good package. Not as insulting as the package the Phillies got for Curt Schilling [Arizona sent Omar Daal, Nelson Figueroa, Travis Lee, and Vicente Padilla to Philadelphia in exchange for Schilling]. But when Flood said no, then that took the cherry off the sundae, so to speak.

"They wound up getting Garry Maddox, a Gold Glove center fielder. The one rap on Flood was that he played so damn deep. But Maddox played extremely shallow and cut off the alleys like a windshield wiper. Willie Montanez was the player the Phillies got from St. Louis when Flood didn't report. He was a very popular player who got them Maddox from San Francisco a few years later."

Curt Flood would challenge baseball's reserve clause. While the swift center fielder would have perhaps the biggest impact on baseball in the history of the sport, his challenge to baseball's reserve clause and the power of the clubs was not the first. But it certainly was the most damaging.

4

THE RESERVE CLAUSE

The Challenge from South of the Border

What exactly is the reserve clause? For decades and decades, the following paragraphs for renewal, the reserve clause, have been part of a player's standard contract.

10. (a) On or before February 1st (or if a Sunday, then the next preceding business day) of the year next following the last played season covered by this contract, the Club may tender to the Player a contract for the term of that year by mailing the same to the Player at his address following his signature hereto, or if none be given, then at his last address of record with the Club. If prior to the March 1 next succeeding said February 1, the Player and the Club have not agreed upon the terms of such contract, then on or before 10 days after said March 1, the Club shall have the right by written notice to the Player at said address to renew this contact for the period of one year on the same terms, except that the amount payable to the player shall be such as the Club shall fix in said notice; provided, however, that said amount, if fixed by a Major League Club, shall be an amount payable at a rate not less than 75 percent of the rate stipulated for the preceding year.

(b) The Club's right to renew this contract, as provided in subparagraph (a) of this paragraph 10, and the promise of the Player not to play otherwise than with the Club have been taken into consideration in determining the amount payable under paragraph 2 hereof.

Those two run-on paragraphs were at the heart of the business of baseball for many years and were always a source of heartache and pain for a huge majority of the players. The extent to which organized baseball could control the game and its players represented a raw nerve for the players that grew more uncomfortable with every year that passed.

Over the years, there had been attempts to circumvent baseball's reserve clause. Since its inception in 1879 and when it was written into the standard player's contract in 1887, the reserve clause gave owners a vice-grip on the players by totally controlling their movement. There was no free agency and players went where they were told to go, or they went to work.

"What the reserve clause brought in was that the players were now controlled," said author Jerrold Casway. "The collusion of the owners to protect their investment and property is how they determine the fate of a ballplayer. That only worked because of the tacit agreement amongst the owners that they would all recognize the rights and responsibility of each other and they would not violate that. The onus was not on the player."

The power amassed by Major League Baseball over its players was largely due to a decision made in the Supreme Court in 1922. In the case of *Federal Baseball Club of Baltimore v. National League of Professional Clubs*, Supreme Court justice Oliver Wendell Holmes created an exemption for professional baseball from the application of antitrust laws. The Baltimore team, which was a member of the Federal League, had filed suit because that organization deemed their inability to sign players was due to antitrust violations. Any business that operates across state borders and participates in interstate commerce is subject to antitrust legislation. Any attempt to control or monopolize trade may be illegal under the Sherman and Clayton Acts.

The Holmes decision was based on the determination that baseball did not involve interstate commerce and as a result federal courts did not have the power to regulate it.

Speaking for a unanimous Court, Holmes concluded that baseball was a business involved in giving exhibitions, which are purely state affairs. The Court also held that baseball was not commerce. While teams played in different states and equipment had to cross state lines, the exhibition was not trade or commerce in the commonly accepted use of those words. The transportation of players and equipment across state lines was deemed merely incidental to the business conducted at baseball parks.

In the ensuing years, the Supreme Court broadened the idea of what interstate commerce was with relation to sports and entertainment. The Court never overturned the ruling in favor of Federal Baseball since owners had made investment decisions based on the belief that organized baseball was in fact exempt from antitrust laws. The Court also invited Congress to enact legislation specific to the application of antitrust laws to baseball. This decision supported the owners' position with regard to the reserve clause and greatly increased their power base.

Over the years, there were attempts to circumvent the control the owners enjoyed by the formulation of new leagues, such as the Players League and the Western League, which morphed into the American League. But while it ultimately failed, it was the Mexican League that shook organized baseball in 1946.

Founded by Ernesto Carmona and Alejandro Aguilar Reyes in 1924, the Mexican League consisted of teams representing eight cities: Mexico City, Puebla, Monterrey, San Luis Potosi, Torreon, Tampico, Nuevo Laredo, and Veracruz. A pair of wealthy brothers who owned banks, newspapers, and even the national lottery,

Jorge and Bernardo Pasquel tried to compete with Major League Baseball.

The owner of the Veracruz Azules, Jorge Pasquel, wanted to put the Mexican League on a par with its Northern neighbors, the major leagues. It was during an accidental meeting Pasquel had with New York Giants player Danny Gardella at a New York gymnasium that the seeds of his plan may have been planted. Pasquel could not believe that a player of Gardella's stature would have to work a regular job during the off-season. He literally offered Gardella a job in the Mexican League on the spot, which he refused. But the die was cast.

The following spring, Gardella was involved in a contract dispute with the Giants and also had a squabble with the team's traveling secretary, Eddie Brannick. The Giants wanted him to accept a $5,000 salary, just $500 more than he was paid in 1945 when he hit .272 with eighteen home runs and seventy-two RBIs. Gardella thought his production had earned him a higher price tag for the following season. At that time he contacted Pasquel, and on February 18 accepted an offer of $8,000 for the season in direct violation of the reserve clause, which provided stability for the owners by preventing a bidding war and free movement by the players. Unlike other players who followed, Gardella did not jump his contract. His move to Mexico was in contrast to the owners' belief that the reserve clause automatically allowed them to renew a player's contract. So unlike the players who walked out on their clubs, Gardella would ultimately represent a serious challenge to the reserve clause.

Upon his arrival in Mexico, Gardella told reporters that "I do not intend to let the Giants enrich themselves at my expense, by selling me to a minor league club after the shabby treatment they have accorded me. So I have now decided to take my gifted talents to Mexico."

The league south of the border began to entice major league players to jump from their American teams to Mexican clubs,

Danny Gardella challenged the reserve clause.
National Baseball Hall of Fame Library, Cooperstown, NY.

strictly against the guidelines of the reserve clause, or even to walk out on existing contracts. While they didn't attract any huge stars, the Pasquel brothers were able to lure some decent players. In addition to Gardella, Dolph Camilli, Mickey Owen, Luis Olmo, Alex Carrasquel, Ace Adams, Harry Feldman, Adrian Zabala, and Vern Stephens soon signed on the dotted line.

Some better-known players such as Max Lanier, Fred Martin (6-0 with St. Louis after six starts), and Lou Klein signed in May of 1946. While the brothers failed in their efforts to land such stars as Ted Williams and Stan Musial, they certainly can't be accused of not throwing money at such stars. They offered Bob Feller $120,000 per year for three years, but he declined. They offered Stan Musial $175,000 a year for five years. He declined. They offered Ted Williams $500,000 to sign and what amounted to a blank check for his salary. When the Splendid Splinter asked if the Mexican League would allow him to have four strikes in every at bat, while the rest of the planet had but three, they agreed. He did not.

At one point the St. Louis Cardinals organization was so unhappy with having its roster raided by the Pasquel brothers that the owner of the club, Sam Breadon, took matters into his own hands. Ignoring an edict from Commissioner Chandler, he flew to Mexico City and met with the Pasquels and convinced them to stop signing his players. Breadon may have stopped the bleeding caused by the Mexican League, but Chandler fined him $5,000 because he was concerned about one team making a deal with the Mexicans that would not apply to the remainder of the major league teams.

Why would major league players risk their careers for an unproven commodity such as the Mexican League? The simple fact of the matter is that baseball players didn't make much money and saw this rogue league as a way to earn more money and have some say in their destiny.

"You had no leverage when talking contract with the organization," said Tim McCarver, a catcher for four decades, now an author and broadcaster. "You thought you were worth more money, but you had nobody representing you. They had you by the nape of the neck and there wasn't anything you could do except hold out."

A number of black players who had been banned from the big leagues for years also got to play in the Mexican League, including Satchel Paige, Josh Gibson, Leon Day, Willard Brown, and Ray Dandridge. The Mexican League teams were able to attract some fine ballplayers from north of the border. But such behavior resulted in pressure from Major League Baseball, as well as financial concerns internally and resentment among many of the long-term players in the league.

Major League Baseball did not sit idly by as this serious threat continued. Commissioner Happy Chandler announced that any player who jumped his contract or violated the reserve status by signing on with a team in the Mexican League would be banned from baseball for five years, unless he rejoined his team by opening day of the 1946 season. That threat proved effective because while five years is not a long time over the span of a lifetime, in terms of a baseball career, five years could be an eternity.

"The question was having the penalty severe enough so that it would deter fellas who might want to do the same thing for quick money," Chandler said while explaining how his penalty would act as a deterrent to keep more players from jumping ship. "I just made it five years and stopped a whole lot of them."

As mentioned previously, the spending frenzy of Jorge Pasquel and his fellow owners took its toll economically. Thanks to the enormous contracts being paid out to major league players, the Mexican League now had to depend on attendance and gate receipts to have the ultimate impact on the bottom line. Teams such as Puebla struggled and resentment continued due to the big salaries paid to the American players. While the new players were used to a certain degree of professionalism in the game, they found the Mexican League wanting in many areas. For the most part, ballparks were in horrendous condition, often lacking the simplest of necessities such as a clubhouse and shower. The stands were uncomfortable and cramped and the fields were atrocious; bad hops were the norm on balding, bumpy, unkept playing surfaces.

When it came to the Mexican League the honeymoon for the American players was over almost before it began. But the death knell for the league and its big-league dreams was probably the loss of Mickey Owen, who had jumped the Brooklyn Dodgers to play for and manage Veracruz.

As the skipper of the team and catcher, Owen, a nine-year big-league veteran, was almost always interfered with by Jorge Pasquel, who often appeared on the field, sometimes in uniform, to undermine Owen's instructions to his players. According to William Marshall's book, *Baseball's Pivotal Era, 1945–1951*, by midsummer, Owen was just plain homesick, particularly when he discovered that his former Dodger teammates were in the midst of the National League pennant race, in spite of having two inexperienced backstops on the team.

In addition, he wanted desperately to respond to the countless questions he was receiving from major league players who wanted to learn about the Mexican League and if they should consider following in Owen's footsteps. But he could not admit that he had made what he termed "the mistake of my life."

By July, he had endured all he could. He sent his young son home and then with the help of a Mexican taxi driver, he crossed the border at Brownsville with his wife. The Mexican League was angry about his departure and even more unhappy about disparaging comments he made about Mexican hospitality, food, and playing conditions. Suffice to say that Mickey Owen did not have a favorable reputation in Mexico. In fact, in September of 1946, Pasquel filed a $127,000 suit against the catcher. Owen pleaded to be reinstated to the commissioner. But Chandler replied that he could find "no good reason" why the catcher's request should be granted.

The comments made by Owen, along with Commissioner Chandler's hard-line stance against any player who fled to Mexico as an alternative to the major leagues, doomed the upstart league. It folded in 1948. But that was only a stepping stone in the situation for the players who were blacklisted. With the demise of the Mexican League and a five-year banishment from the major leagues, the players who had jumped leagues had nowhere to go.

With no other alternative available, a number of players filed suit against Major League Baseball in an effort to be reinstated and allowed to continue their playing careers in the major leagues.

Gardella played baseball in Quebec and also worked as a hospital orderly in New York, but he desperately wanted to return to the major leagues. Missing all of 1947 because of the Chandler ban, Gardella filed a federal suit against Major League Baseball for $300,000 in damages. A law school classmate of Chandler, Frederic Johnson, was Gardella's lawyer and was anxious to test the reserve clause, especially since Gardella had not broken his contract. He had a particularly strong case.

On July 14, 1948, U.S. district judge Henry Goddard dismissed the case, agreeing with baseball that America's Pastime was amusement, rather than interstate commerce. Gardella appealed the case to the U.S. Court of Appeals, which reversed the dismissal and ordered the case to trial.

Lanier and Martin dropped their litigation on June 5, 1949, when Commissioner Chandler, "to temper justice with mercy," lifted the suspensions against all of the players who went to Mexico and gave them permission to return to Major League Baseball. But it has always been thought that the real reason that baseball lifted the bans was not mercy, but a calculated attempt to keep legal challenges to the reserve clause out of the courts for fear that it would lose. Many representatives of organized baseball feared that the end of the reserve clause would result in the end of professional baseball.

Gardella did not withdraw his suit even after he was allowed reinstatement into Major League Baseball. The case went so far that Commissioner Chandler was actually deposed by Frederic Johnson. But in a shocking turn of events that fall during the World Series, Gardella announced that he was dropping his lawsuit and would resume his major league career with the St. Louis Cardinals. Years later, in 1961, Gardella admitted that he was given

$60,000 from baseball to withdraw his suit. About half of his settlement went to his legal fees.

The court cases would have been interesting since the players, except Gardella, knew that they had breached their contracts by jumping to the new league. But their legal stance was that the contracts were illegal because they represented an illegal restraint of trade or commerce and promoted a monopoly for organized baseball.

In 1953, baseball won yet another court battle as a career minor league player named George Toolson brought suit against the New York Yankees and baseball's reserve system because he believed that the reserve clause kept him from having the opportunity to play for another major league team. The suit reached the U.S. Supreme Court, which ruled in a split decision once again that baseball, even with radio and television sending games all across the country, did not constitute interstate commerce. In rejecting Toolson's appeal, the court shifted the burden to Congress to overturn baseball's antitrust exemption.

But a slow change seemed to be taking place. Gardella had perhaps the strongest case of any in challenging the reserve clause and Toolson had his case heard by the Supreme Court. Even though he lost, it was by a split decision. It would still take many years for baseball's reserve clause to meet its match.

5

THE RESERVE CLAUSE

The Challenge from Curt Flood

As the 1970 season approached, it became more obvious with every passing day that Curt Flood was not going to report to the Philadelphia Phillies. He was so adamant in his desire to dictate where he would play that he was willing to give up an annual salary of $100,000. Even though Phillies general manager John Quinn left a meeting with Flood feeling that he had convinced the center fielder to report to the team, the players' union and its head, Marvin Miller, advised Flood that the union was prepared to pay the cost of a lawsuit, should he decide to file an antitrust suit against organized baseball.

On Christmas Eve of 1969, two and a half months after the trade was made, Flood sent a letter to the late commissioner of baseball, Bowie Kuhn, demanding his freedom. The letter read, in part:

"After twelve years in the major leagues, I do not feel I am a piece of property to be bought and sold irrespective of my wishes. I believe that any system which produces that result violates my basic rights as a citizen and is inconsistent with the laws of the United States and of the several States.

"It is my desire to play baseball in 1970 and I am capable of playing. I have received a contract offer from the Philadelphia club, but I believe I have the right to consider offers from other clubs before making any decision. I, therefore, request that you make known to all Major League clubs my feeling in this matter, and advise them of my availability for the 1970 season."

Not surprisingly, his request was denied based on the reserve clause and its inclusion of Flood's 1969 contract. While he toyed with the idea of retirement, on January 16, 1970, Flood filed a $4.1 million lawsuit against Kuhn and Major League Baseball. Even though he was assuredly losing a number of seasons at a six-figure salary, Curt Flood had to take a stand, understanding that this in all probability marked the end of his brilliant playing career. Teammates and friends went out of their way to make sure that the talented outfielder knew the stakes of taking such a stand.

"All of his friends were very helpful in trying to get him to realize what he was doing," said Flood's long-time St. Louis teammate Tim McCarver, who was also involved in the trade to the Phillies. "What many of them didn't realize was that he didn't need any help. He knew what he was doing."

When Flood was discussing the case at a meeting with members of the Major League Baseball Players Association, led by Marvin Miller, he stated as clearly as he could why he was taking this stand.

"I want you to know that what I'm doing here I'm doing as a ballplayer, a major league ballplayer, and I think it is absolutely terrible that we have stood by and watched this situation go on for so many years and never pulled together to do anything about it," he said. "It's improper, it shouldn't be allowed to go any further and the circumstances are such that, well, I guess this is the time to do something."

Flood also understood why it would be so difficult for the average baseball fan to have empathy for his stance against Major League Baseball. He once said, "It was difficult for the fans to

Curt Flood sacrificed his career.
National Baseball Hall of Fame Library, Cooperstown, NY.

understand my problems with baseball. I was telling my story to deaf ears, because I was telling my story to a person who would give their first-born child to be doing what I was doing."

And what Curt Flood was doing was shaking the foundation of Major League Baseball. While there had been numerous chal-

lenges to the reserve clause in previous years, never had a player
of Flood's stature been willing to walk away from hundreds of
thousands of dollars to make his point. He was a star.

"Some of the owners contend it [the end of the reserve clause]
will end baseball," Flood said. "The 600 players say we'll have a
chance to make more money. I'm not trying to create chaos or end
baseball. I just want to stand up like a human being. I want something we can live with."

Deep in his heart, Curt Flood felt that the reserve clause was
degrading. Flood cited an example in an article he wrote for *Sport*
magazine in 1970.

"I never had to look beyond the Cardinal clubhouse, or my own
locker, to see how the reserve clause degraded us all," he wrote.
"One Sunday afternoon in a game against New York, I tried to
break up a double play. The Mets' little short stop, Bud Harrelson,
tried to get out of my way, but he landed on my leg with his spikes.
He cut a 10-inch wound from my knee to my thigh. They patched
me up and I finished the game.

"After the game, they put stitches on the wound and gave me
an anti-tetanus shot. The shot knocked me loopy and all night long
I was nauseous and dizzy, the leg stiff and painful. I finally got to
sleep at six in the morning.

"I knew that the Cardinals had scheduled a banquet for noon
the next day and all the players were supposed to be there. But
since the Cardinals knew how sick I'd been in the clubhouse, I was
sure I wasn't expected to attend.

"I got up about two in the afternoon and arrived at the park at
around 3:30 or so. I found a note on my locker to see the general
manager. When I walked into his office, he said, 'Missing that banquet will cost you $250.' 'You don't understand,' I said. I had
already undressed to my shorts, and I showed him the stitched-up
leg. 'No excuses,' he said. I paid the $250."

Flood and his attorney, Arthur Goldberg, made their case,
which eventually made its way to the Supreme Court. In the long

history of baseball, collusion was not a four-letter word; it was a way of life. The argument was made that the Thirteenth Amendment to the Constitution and the Sherman Antitrust Act were violated by the reserve clause. Players, economists, and others testified in favor of Flood and his crusade. Baseball continued its age-old tradition of steadfastly stating that the reserve clause was in place for the good of the game. How could the reserve clause be in violation of the Thirteenth Amendment when the players were more than capable of finding other employment, they asked?

The owners contended that free agency would destroy the game and forever change it from the pastime that generations of fans had come to know and love. The good of the game was their mantra and the reserve clause was clearly for the good of the game.

Federal judge Ben Cooper ruled against Curt Flood on August 12, 1970, reaffirming the reserve clause, but noting that players and owners should negotiate the issue. The U.S. Court of Appeals also rejected Flood. Eventually the Supreme Court ruled in 1972 in a 5-3 decision.

"That was the *Brown v. The Board of Education* of baseball," said Bill Conlin. "There were far-sweeping effects even though Curt Flood lost the Supreme Court decision. It had a profound snowball effect on the entire labor picture in Major League Baseball to the extent that the big thing the justices did was to tell baseball that the reserve clause was not a matter to be decided by a point of law, but by collective bargaining between the players and the owners.

"It made perfect sense that Curt Flood would be the person to challenge baseball. He was a very proud individual. And I think he knew who he was and what he wanted to do. He had established a business in St. Louis, as well as the thriving portrait business he was involved with. He felt very strongly about the concept that he was not a piece of property that could be sold or traded to another city without his approval. He was a very principled guy."

Any baseball discussion about Marvin Miller will almost always line up team owners solidly against the union leader and players uniformly behind him. He is not held in much regard at all on one side and walks on water on the other. Miller made a name for himself in labor representation during the years he spent with the United Steel Workers of America and the United Automobile Workers. Few realize that he loved baseball and was a die-hard Brooklyn Dodgers fan who idolized pitcher Dazzy Vance.

Any discussion of Marvin Miller will also include information about how the average salary of a Major League Baseball player rose from $6,000 when he took control of the Major League Baseball Players Association in 1966 to $500,000 when he left in 1984.

Writer Red Smith once wrote, "When you speak of Babe Ruth, he is one of the two men, in my opinion, who changed baseball the most. The second most influential man in the history of baseball is Marvin Miller." No matter on which side of the aisle you might find yourself, it is difficult to argue Smith's claim.

Bill Giles, chairman of the Philadelphia Phillies, has been involved in baseball for his entire life. The son of former Cincinnati owner and National League president Warren Giles, he has the unique perspective not only of his lifetime, but of his father's as well.

"My dad felt strongly about the reserve clause and was anti-Marvin Miller," Bill Giles said. "He would always speak about how Miller was so bad for baseball. He felt that it would be hard to make money because the cost of labor would go up. My dad was right.

"He said that if we lost the reserve clause it would destroy baseball. It would be a disincentive to building farm systems."

Needless to say, the other side is just as adamant.

"I didn't know about the reserve clause or any of those things," said Tim McCarver. "I was seventeen years old when I came up. It never crossed my mind until I met Marvin Miller. What the owners failed to realize in those days was that they were dealing with a group of professional competitors. Even though we were naïve and ignorant of the machinations that went on, we cared about the pension plan and we cared about our contracts. It was Marvin Miller who made the players' association lucid and educated. That's what he did, he educated us. And with education came resolve. With resolve came unity and that led to one of the best unions on the Earth."

During the Flood lawsuit, the owners made a huge error when they agreed that the idea of the reserve clause should not be decided in the courts. Rather, it should be a collective bargaining issue that could be decided through negotiation. Removing the reserve clause from the standard player contract was the major goal of the players' union in their negotiations with the owners. And the players were a determined group, with a charismatic leader in Miller.

While the players may have lost the battle in the Flood case, they ultimately won the war because of his selfless efforts. That is a fact that has not been lost on generations of baseball players who have enjoyed the freedom of movement in baseball that Curt Flood only dreamed of.

"Even though Curt Flood lost his Supreme Court case against baseball's reserve clause, he still earned the respect of the players for the way he stood up and fought for what he believed in," wrote Mike Schmidt in his book, *Clearing the Bases*. "Curt Flood never reaped any reward for his stand against Major League Baseball. He understood that what he was doing was for the players of the future. I wonder how many of today's players know the story of Curt Flood? Or what Andy Messersmith and Dave McNally did for them? Or the risks the early leaders of the MLBPA ran in standing up to the owners? Or the huge role played by Marvin Miller in transforming baseball—and our lives—by ending business as usual? These men made possible my salary, my security, and all that followed.

"Conduct a poll of athletes in the big four professional team sports today. Ask them just one question: Who was Curt Flood?

"How many do you think could correctly identify him as the man who sacrificed his career to make theirs possible?"

Other former players also understand the impact of Curt Flood on the game of baseball and the eventual advent of free agency, which also drastically changed the way that baseball trades are made.

"There's no doubt in my mind that Curt's actions got the ball rolling from freeing players from a ninety-year clause that could tie them to a team against their wills," said Tim McCarver. "Those million-dollar contracts of today exist in large part due to Curt Flood."

The difference between the game of that generation and the game of today is stunning. While the owners held a tight reign over the game, in recent decades it is the players who have won nearly all of the labor battles and who now enjoy the fruits of those labors. How far the players have come is still sometimes hard to believe.

"We were signed into perpetuity back in the '60s with a one-year contract forever," said Rick Wise, whose eighteen-year major league career saw him pitch for the Phillies, Cardinals, Red Sox, Indians, and Padres, amassing a 188-181 record. "That's what Curt Flood fought about. I had a tremendous amount of respect for his ability as a player, but he was also a first-class gentleman. He was the right person at the right time. I had been a player representative a couple of times and also an alternate. But he was the man who initiated this on behalf of all players.

"Some of today's players know about what he did, but I really doubt that they know the history of the game. Not just the economics of the game, or the strife between players and management. But a lot of them don't even know the history of their game."

While more experienced players may have discussed the reserve clause among themselves before Curt Flood made his historic stance by not reporting to Philadelphia, most young players didn't know the reserve clause from Santa Claus. Realistically, who could blame them? The goal was to earn a spot on a big-league roster. Then, the even tougher proposition of keeping that roster spot was their main focus. To be aware of the ramifications of a small clause that was part of every player's contract for more than ninety years was asking a bit much.

"I think I was like every other young player at the time," said Larry Colton, a fine minor league pitcher who made one appearance in the major leagues and has since become a Pulitzer Prize–nominated author. "All I wanted to do was play and make it to the big leagues. The idea of free agency never occurred to me. I didn't feel like a piece of beef, or some indentured servant. I didn't know any better. It wasn't something we talked about. Even though I was from Berkeley and the whole concept of free expression was blossoming on campus, it didn't transfer to my world in baseball. If Willie Mays and Don Drysdale couldn't switch teams, why would I think I could?

"None of the players had agents back then. And nobody discussed salaries. We didn't know what the other players were making and the organization liked it that way. I made $500 a month my first year in the game and $8,000 when I made the big leagues. I thought I was living large, even though I was always broke and had to take off-season jobs. I worked for 3M, Jack LaLane, a sporting goods company, and did public relations for the California Seals hockey team. I played winter ball in Puerto Rico one year. Reserve clause . . . what was that? But in 1969 Marvin Miller came and spoke to us in spring training. That's the first hint I had that something was up. But still, my goal was to make the Show, not make lots of money.

"What Curt Flood did was bold, brave, and beneficial for the players. I didn't know him personally when I played, but I was in Philly for an old-timers game about ten years ago and wandered into the hotel bar and sat down next to him. I didn't recognize him. We struck up a conversation and I asked him if he was in town on business. 'I'm here for an old-timers game,' he said modestly.

When he told me his name, I about fell off my stool. Then I spent the next twenty minutes genuflecting. The next day I had my picture in the paper with him and Bob Feller. Two legends and a Larry."

While many big-league players may not have been aware of baseball's journey toward player freedom at the beginning of their careers, most were able to learn with some on-the-job training. Make no mistake; they appreciate the efforts made on their behalf. And many of the players who have seen their lives made better because of the efforts of Curt Flood are very appreciative.

"As a young player I had no idea about the reserve clause," said Jim Gott, who pitched for fourteen major league seasons with the Blue Jays, Giants, Pirates, and Dodgers. "I just thought that was how it was. I was just trying to make the ball club. It wasn't until 1985 when I was voted assistant player rep when my education in baseball came. I recommend it for every player in the game. Know who fought for you and how precious these things are.

"Curt Flood gave me an opportunity to have some savings in my bank account right now and help make the transition from baseball to public life much easier. Curt Flood was the Jackie Robinson of the game from the financial standpoint of the players. I never met him, but I went to his funeral and paid my respects to him. I've heard former players talk about the talented person he was on the field, how much culture he had and what a great guy he was. He significantly changed the financial aspect of the game. Now guys can move around from team to team, which they could not do before. It's a much better situation than the players had in the generation before me."

After his dramatic suit was heard by the Supreme Court, Curt Flood did return to baseball. He sat out the 1970 season and that November he was traded by the Phillies to the Washington Senators along with a player to be named later (Jeff Terpko) in exchange for Greg Goossen, Gene Martin, and, in a strange twist of fate, Jeff Terpko.

Former pitcher Jim Gott.
Courtesy of the Los Angeles Dodgers.

Flood signed a contract with the Senators for $110,000 but played in only thirteen games for Washington, hitting just .200. Because he had missed so much time, the game had passed him by and he was unable to play at the level he had become so accustomed to. He died in 1997 in Los Angeles. In another irony, a year after his death, Congress passed what is known as the Curt Flood Act of 1998, which changed baseball's antitrust exemption to state that professional baseball players would be covered under general antitrust laws without affecting the game's exemption.

"What he did led to the changes in the reserve system," said Tal Smith, of the Houston Astros. "Historically, it is one of the most important things in the annals of the game."

While Flood lost his case, it forced owners to accept collective bargaining in their negotiations with the players. Just three years after the Flood case reached the Supreme Court, the reserve clause was about to be undone, forever changing how Major League Baseball players changed teams. For the first time, the choice was about to be theirs.

In later years, Flood spoke about Augie Busch and his years with the Cardinals. There was no trace of bitterness. But his words make one wonder what would have happened if the St. Louis Cardinals had treated Flood like a valued contributor to their success when attempting to trade him.

"Mr. Busch treated us like sons," Flood said. "There is absolutely nothing negative I can say about being here [in St. Louis], about playing here all those years. We were a family and I was not really angry, but I was a little unhappy. We had won three consecutive pennants and two World Series and it hurt me that they thought so little of what we did together. I guess there is a nice way to tell a guy they don't need him anymore."

6

THE RESERVE CLAUSE

The Challenge from Messersmith and McNally:
Walking the Walk

While you can't call Curt Flood's battle against baseball a victory for him personally, it was most certainly the major development that led to free agency for major league players. The owners agreed that the reserve clause was an issue to be decided in collective bargaining with the players and not in the courts. That proved to be a disastrous decision from management's point of view.

The owners began to give in, but not without a strong public stance and the same type of attitude they exhibited when they were the czars of the game. An agreement struck with the players in 1973 led to final-offer salary arbitration, which allowed players with just two years of major league experience to have salary disputes decided by an impartial arbitrator.

The entire arbitration process can be difficult, as the arbitrator listens to arguments from both sides, including information about the player's performance as well as the salaries earned by players deemed to be similar in production. Then, either the figure offered by the team or the one asked for by the player is chosen.

Often, a team will opt to pay a player a higher salary than it might ordinarily in order to avoid the arbitration hearing, which can be harmful to the relationship between the organization and the player.

Before the landmark case of 1975, there were a number of near-misses where players came close to playing a season without a contract. In 1972, Cardinals catcher Ted Simmons rejected a St. Louis contract offer but chose not to hold out. He wanted to get in shape for the season and showed up at spring training, forcing the team to renew his contract. Any thought of Simmons being the player to test the reserve clause in front of an arbitrator ended when he signed a two-year contract on July 24 of that year.

According to *The Sporting News Official Baseball Guide, 1974*, as many as seven players opened the season playing with renewed contracts they did not sign. The players included Stan Bahnsen, Rick Reichardt, and Mike Andrews of the Chicago White Sox, Jim Kaat of Minnesota, Dick Billings of Texas, Fritz Peterson of the Yankees, and Jerry Kenney of Cleveland.

Kaat signed with the Twins just before the regular season began. Bahnsen, Billings, and Peterson all signed contracts during the year and Kenney, Reichardt, and Andrews were all released.

In 1975, the owners made another critical mistake. Pitchers Andy Messersmith, of the Los Angeles Dodgers, and Dave McNally, of the Montreal Expos, both refused to sign their contracts for the season. The teams forced the players to report and renewed their contracts, as the reserve clause stipulates. That they played a season without a signed contract convinced the players that both pitchers were free agents. Marvin Miller even attempted to give the owners an opportunity to make changes to the reserve clause. But their imperial attitude remained and they refused.

"This was a very important happening because this was the first time the players really took on the owners," said Jerrold Casway. "Had the owners given the players just a little more freedom and respect, you would not have had the Flood situation, the unions,

Andy Messersmith was just what the players needed.
Courtesy of the Los Angeles Dodgers.

and the strikes. From the 1903 merger of the two leagues up until the Curt Flood incident, the owners did exactly what they wanted to do. On each occasion, the owners put their foot in their mouth and either overreacted or underreacted."

That was about to change. Unlike Curt Flood, Andy Messersmith was not considering giving up his baseball career. He wanted to continue his career, but continue it on his terms. That was against all that the baseball hierarchy believed in and was used to. They had never lost a battle up to this point and saw no reason to believe this case would be any different.

"This was very significant," said Fred Claire. "It really had to do with the reserve clause and ultimately played a part as far as free agency and the collective bargaining agreement. It changed the structure of the game relative to free agency.

"Andy Messersmith was someone I knew very well and was close to. Andy loved pitching for the Dodgers and did not want to leave. He wanted a no-trade clause in his contract and did not get it. This was a major factor in free agency. Flood, Messersmith, and McNally drastically changed the game because they gave management less control and gave the players more control."

Messersmith came off a 20-6 season in 1974 and responded with a 19-14 campaign for the Dodgers in 1975, solidifying his position as one of the best pitchers in the major leagues. McNally went just 3-6 with Montreal, the final year of a brilliant fourteen-year career that saw him finish with a 184-119 record. But the plight of these two veteran hurlers was not necessarily about success on the baseball diamond in 1975. It was their position off the field that took precedence.

At the conclusion of the season, Marvin Miller persuaded both Messersmith and McNally to file grievances against Major League Baseball to challenge the system. With these two pitchers at the forefront of the battle, the union argued that a contract could be renewed for only one year. After that, a player was free to sign on with any other club, which was directly in opposition to the owners' belief that the reserve clause allowed contracts to be extended and renewed indefinitely.

Clearly, the willingness of these two players to challenge baseball's reserve clause led to the most defining arbitration decision in the history of baseball, if not the history of all sports. It may have been the biggest victory in the history of the labor movement. While Messersmith has refused to comment on his place in baseball history in recent years, he did express his feelings to *New York Times* writer Murray Chase in a February 1976 article.

"I'm not a martyr, but I wouldn't change anything," he said.

"I've gained a lot of notoriety, but I don't want it. That's not why I did this. It was done for selfish reasons but also for some unselfish reasons. A lot of things had to be changed, and this is the way it has to be done.

"It had to be a veteran player, someone who was established and who would still be playing. It couldn't be a guy who was finished and no one would want."

Thanks to the agreement concerning arbitration, the case went in front of a three-man panel that included Marvin Miller, John Gaherin (the owners' representative), and chairman Peter Seitz. In another case where the worst enemy of the owners was their own combative attitudes, Seitz even told the owners that the players held most of the cards in this case and that they should try to negotiate a settlement with the players on the issue of the reserve clause. But the owners refused.

"I think that probably the ownership side was too stubborn and thought they would remain status quo and that they could maintain the system the way it was," said Pat Gillick. "Even before those decisions came down there was some encouragement by the arbitrator to get both sides to settle it. Maybe they could have reached some common ground. But ownership was too stubborn and thought they would maintain the status quo."

But before the final verdict was reached, as the players of the arbitration case were being chosen, there were some who objected to Peter Seitz being involved as the arbitrator. Seitz had been involved with a number of salary arbitrations between players and their clubs in the past. That experience had some people on the ownership side of the equation feeling queasy about having such an important hearing chaired by Peter Seitz.

Between his stints with the Houston Astros, Tal Smith was working with the New York Yankees. He and general manager Gabe Paul worked together in the Yankees organization and had sat across the table from Peter Seitz. Their experience with the arbitrator began in the years before Andy Messersmith and Dave McNally tested the system.

"That whole case was rather interesting," said Smith. "I had done salary arbitration for the Yankees for four players in 1974. The players were Bill Sudakis, Wayne Granger, Duke Sims, and Gene Michael. At least one of those hearings was in front of Peter Seitz, but I can't remember exactly which one it was.

"One day Gabe Paul called me into his office when he was on a conference call with John Gaherin, when they were discussing selecting an arbitrator. Gabe and I both urged them not to put this case in the hands of Seitz. I didn't have a lot of confidence in Seitz's understanding of baseball. Both Gabe and I argued it. I just think that Seitz was not well informed with baseball issues. He was very liberal. It was just not something I felt comfortable with."

The concern felt by Gabe Paul and Tal Smith was well-founded. But baseball once again turned a deaf ear to their warning and paid the ultimate price. In the most stunning verdict ever struck with regard to baseball's reserve clause, after both pitchers submitted the grievance to arbitration, on December 23, 1975, arbitrator Seitz declared that the Major League Baseball player's contract bound them to a team for only one year after the prior contract expired. This decision took the teeth out of the reserve clause, effectively ending the power and control that the reserve clause had given the owners.

"The grievances of Messersmith and McNally are sustained," Peter Seitz wrote in his decision. "There is no contractual bond between these players and the Los Angeles and the Montreal clubs, respectively. Absent such a contract, their clubs had no right or power, under the Basic Agreement, the uniform player contract of the Major League Rules, to reserve their services for their exclusive use for any period beyond the 'renewal year' in the contracts which these players had heretofore signed with their clubs."

Strike one.

In spite of the ruling by Seitz, baseball was not about to roll over and simply accept the decision. It appealed to the U.S. District Court for Western Missouri, but the Seitz ruling was upheld in February of 1976 by judge John Oliver.

Strike two.

Later, the Eighth Circuit Court of Appeals also upheld the ruling.

Strike three. The owners were out. The players and their union had hit the ultimate walk-off home run and had wrestled control of their own destiny away from the owners. While the ultimate agreement concerning free agency was fair to the owners, it would forever change the face of the game.

Following the full extent of appeals, Major League Baseball and the players' association negotiated and agreed that players with six years of experience could become free agents. The teams that lost free agents would only receive amateur draft picks in exchange. While the reserve clause still exists in baseball contracts, it has no bearing on the comings and goings of players as it did in the past.

"After Curt Flood, the next step was to get into the system they have now, where a federal arbitrator who was agreed upon by both sides was set up," said columnist Bill Conlin. "Then we had the famous McNally and Messersmith case, where they in effect sued for their free agency. Peter Seitz, who was called a communist by the writer Dick Young, declared them free agents. Nothing has ever been the same since then."

Andy Messersmith never wanted to leave the Dodgers. It was his inability to have a no-trade clause written into his contract that was behind the stance he took. When the Dodgers finally did make him a no-trade offer, it was too late. The lines had been drawn in the sand.

The Atlanta Braves won the Andy Messersmith sweepstakes, signing the talented right-hander to a three-year, $1 million contract. Owner Ted Turner tried to make the most of his acquisition by attempting to convince Messersmith to adopt the nickname "Channel" so it could be placed on the back of his uniform along with jersey number 17. In Atlanta, it was Channel 17 that broadcast Braves games. The idea never had a chance as Major League Baseball stepped in.

In 1976, Messersmith went 11-11 with the Braves, but fell to 5-4 in an injury-plagued campaign in 1977. That winter he was purchased by the New York Yankees, where the injury bug continued to follow him. After going 0-3, he was released by New York and signed by the team he never wanted to leave, the Dodgers, for the 1979 season. But he was released after going 2-4 in eleven games.

In another interview with the *New York Times*, Messersmith spoke of how helping put aside the effectiveness of baseball's reserve clause by walking the walk made him a marked man. The guy who had been a popular player with fans was suddenly treated as America's top villain.

"I wasn't prepared for the pressure that came down," he said. "I didn't know anything about it. I came out as the dirty dog. That was a real hard thing for me. I just wasn't ready for it."

While he was much younger at the time, during his college days at Berkeley, Messersmith may have exhibited some of the independence that eventually led to his stance against Major League Baseball. One of his college teammates was pitcher Larry Colton.

"Andy was a freshman when I was a senior in 1964," he said. "Freshmen couldn't play on the varsity back then, so we never actually played together. I did get to know him a little bit, however. I was the ace of the varsity staff, so he was politely respectful. I liked him and invited him by the fraternity. As I recall, I invited him by the house to try to get him to join, but he wanted to stay independent. At that time, joining a frat was allegedly the thing to do, so his decision not to join was perhaps a harbinger of his going outside the box.

"After Andy's rookie year in the bigs, we got together a couple of times in the off-season to play golf. The tables were switched . . . he was on the varsity and I was looking up. He was also a lot better golfer. The last time I saw him was in 2004 when I was on tour for *Counting Coup* [a Pulitzer Prize–nominated book authored by Colton]. He lives near Santa Cruz and we met for lunch. The thing that he told me that struck me the most was how all the big-league teams shunned him after he had challenged the reserve clause. This was despite the fact that he was coming off several really great years. The only team that would give him a chance was Ted Turner and the Braves. Today, teams would be falling all over themselves to give him gobs of money.

"My only claim over Andy is that I still hold the Cal single game record for strikeouts—19—a record I'm sure he'd trade his Cy Young Award for."

Dave McNally lent his name to the effort to show support for the players, even though he had decided to retire from the game sporting a 184-119 record. He was a twenty-game winner from 1968 to 1971 with the Baltimore Orioles. It was in 1971 that McNally and three Oriole teammates, Jim Palmer, Mike Cuellar, and Pat Dobson, all won twenty games.

While he and Messersmith assuredly have made it possible for today's players to earn such astronomical salaries, McNally had a comical comment about the contract that Alex Rodriguez signed with Texas for $252 million.

"My first thought when I saw that was did Texas offer him $250 million and he wanted two more?" McNally asked in the *Billings Gazette*. "How did they get to $252 million?"

After his career ended, McNally owned an auto dealership in Billings, Montana. He died of cancer in 2002. But three years prior to his death, he was named the State Athlete for the Twentieth Century. His comments to the *Gazette* show his love for the game: "That's quite an honor," he said. "Sometimes you forget about the career and then different things come up and bring it all back. It was such a great time. While it was happening, you never think about what you're accomplishing. You're just doing it. And down the road, when not too many people have surpassed what you did, I guess that makes what you accomplished sound a little better."

What was so important about McNally's willingness to challenge the system is that since he had already retired as a player and had no interest in coming back to play again, the owners had no leverage to have him sign a contract. Expos president John McHale, according to McNally, came to his Billings home in November of 1975 offering a $125,000 contract for 1976, along with a signing bonus of $25,000, which was McNally's to keep regardless of whether he pitched again.

Since McNally had no interest in signing a new pact, Los Angeles didn't seriously bother attempting to sign Messersmith because McNally's stance insured that the grievance would be heard.

There is no doubt of Dave McNally's accomplishments on the baseball field. He was one of the premier pitchers of his era. But what he and Andy Messersmith accomplished by walking the walk for all of the players who came before them and all of the players who came afterward changed the game of baseball forever thanks to free agency.

"These were all some pretty gutsy ballplayers that did what they did," said Jim Gott. "We needed those guys to do what they did to help us gain things like no-trade clauses. After Curt Flood, Messersmith and McNally continued to dot the I's and cross the T's, but Flood made it happen. Think of the names of players we never know from before who could have moved on to a different team and gotten a chance to play. We owe these guys a great debt of gratitude."

Only the most serious baseball trivia buff knows that another player spent 1975 playing with a renewed contract. Pittsburgh Pirate Richie Zisk lasted through the season with a renewed contract, but signed with the club just before the start of the playoffs.

"I was with Walter O'Malley [former Los Angeles Dodgers owner] at one point early in the days of free agency," recalled Fred Claire. "He was asked, 'What would Sandy Koufax make if he were pitching today?' Walter spun his cigar and replied, 'He would be my partner.'"

7

ARBITRATION AND FREE AGENCY

Baseball's Brave New World

"Bah humbug" was surely the refrain around the homes of most baseball owners over the Christmas holidays in 1975. What was their world coming to? Arbitrator Peter Seitz had just decided two days earlier that pitchers Andy Messersmith and Dave McNally would be free agents when he rendered the reserve clause, which tied a player to the first team he signed with, impotent. When the owners and players sat down to negotiate a new collective bargaining agreement, the owners had hoped to limit free agency to players with eight years of major league experience. They also wanted any team signing a free agent to compensate the player's former team.

The owners also took the additional step of locking the players out of spring training in 1976. Shortly after the lockout began, commissioner Bowie Kuhn ordered the camps to open, which further infuriated the owners. As America's Game continued on the field, a new collective bargaining agreement was negotiated behind closed doors. Players would gain free agency after six years. After losing a player, the club would be compensated by a draft pick from the signing club. Each free agent could negotiate with his own club and up to twelve others.

The Oakland A's were a team filled with star-quality players, many of which were eligible for free agency. Before the June 15 trading deadline, A's owner Charles O. Finley made deals to avoid losing some of his best players to free agency and getting nothing of value in return. Outfielder Joe Rudi and reliever Rollie Fingers were sold to Boston for $1 million each. The Yankees agreed to pay $1.5 million for overpowering left-handed pitcher Vida Blue. But Kuhn stepped in and vetoed the transactions, saying that they were not in the best interest of baseball.

Just a couple of years before, another top pitcher was granted free agency, but for different reasons. Jim "Catfish" Hunter was the ace of the pitching staff of the Oakland A's. He was made a free agent when the A's failed to make a payment into an insurance annuity that was dictated by his contract. Oakland failed to live up to the contract and lost its best pitcher. As it turned out, that was just a harbinger of things to come. After some very public negotiations, Hunter eventually signed a rich deal with the New York Yankees. As fate would have it, Hunter would be far from the last player to leave Oakland for greener pastures.

But it should be noted that the most powerful influence in the game leading to free agency was not the Messersmith and McNally case, but the system that enabled them to challenge the reserve clause in arbitration rather than a court of law. And arbitration was a system that the owners not only agreed to, but promoted energetically. Ironically, it turned out to be their Waterloo.

The three-year Collective Bargaining Agreement signed in 1970 allowed that disputes not involved in the "integrity of baseball" could be arbitrated by a three-member arbitration panel which was agreed upon jointly by the players and owners. This was a huge distinction for the players, who did not have to present their case before the commissioner of baseball—ultimately an employee of the owners. Now both sides had to present their cases in an environment where justice could actually prevail.

When the CBA was enacted, both sides agreed to table discussions of the reserve clause owing to the pending lawsuit of Curt Flood against Major League Baseball. There is tremendous irony in the fact that it was an impartial arbitrator, Peter Seitz, who would ultimately award the players their free agency. The same free agency that was denied to Curt Flood.

The pendulum continued to swing more to the players even before the Seitz decision. During the collective bargaining agreement negotiations of 1973, the players asked once again for free agency. While that did not happen at that time, players with at least two full seasons in the major leagues earned the right to have their salary determined by an arbitrator. That agreement, which lasted from 1973 to 1975, also granted players the 10/5 rule.

"Free agency is not nearly the burr under the saddle of the owners that arbitration is," said Bill Conlin. "And that is something that they know the players will never give up. One big mistake the owners made was because they were afraid they would get continually hammered by all these court actions. They insisted on a sweeping system of arbitration and players reluctantly agreed to that. The players didn't want it and the owners did. Part of the arbitration process is the current one that killed them so badly. When a player is eligible for arbitration, he can submit his high number and then the owners go low-ball. But the arbitrator can't decide in between. It's one or the other and the owners have been absolutely killed because arbitration has substantially increased salaries. Most owners would gladly get rid of arbitration long before free agency.

"Free agency was inevitable. The owners have a nice window of six years. That's more than the average career of a major league player, which is around three years. That's more than half of the average. So they do have a nice window to control a player that has signed."

The only two clubs who objected to arbitration were St. Louis and Oakland. But the deal was struck and parties on both sides prepared for the first arbitration hearings in the spring of 1974. In February of that year, Minnesota Twins pitcher Dick Woodson won his case, seeking a salary of $29,000. The Twins had offered $23,000.

The results of that first year were a mixed bag. Owners won sixteen of the twenty-nine cases that were heard. That being said, all the players involved received more money than they would have been offered under the old system. The pattern was set. While the owners usually won more cases than they lost, even the players who lost their cases received significant raises.

"One of the worst aspects of the system is that you are forced into competition with your own player," said Bill Giles. "When the team presents its case, it has to devalue the player. This can often lead to hard feelings."

Thanks to the Seitz decision, and no doubt with big bucks in their futures, the players looked forward to enjoying their new-found freedom. In an effort to organize the process, baseball planned a draft for the teams to pick the free agent players they'd like to negotiate with.

On the first of November 1976, some impressive players were declared free agents and became eligible for the inaugural free agent draft. They included eight Oakland A's: Sal Bando, Don Baylor, Bert Campaneris, Nate Colbert, Rollie Fingers, Willie McCovey, Joe Rudi, and Gene Tenace. Baltimore Orioles on the list included Wayne Garland, Bobby Grich, Reggie Jackson, and Royle Stillman. The California Angels lost Paul Dade, Tim Nord-brook, and Billy Smith and Minnesota lost Bill Campbell and Eric Soderholm. The Cubs said goodbye to Steve Stone, the Yankees parted ways with Doyle Alexander, the Phillies lost Dave Cash, Pittsburgh bid adieu to Richie Hebner, and Garry Matthews left the Giants.

The draft was actually an interesting exercise that seemed to work. A team could draft any available player they wanted to negotiate with, but could sign only two players, an effort by baseball to keep the teams with deeper pockets from having an unfair advantage over small-market clubs. Players could be picked by twelve teams, plus their current squad. Once that quota was reached, they were removed from the list of available players. The rule about signing just two players was waived for Oakland, Baltimore, and California, teams that were hit particularly hard by the free agent draft.

At the end of the day, some players had struck it rich. Reggie Jackson left the Orioles to sign a five-year, $400,000-per-year deal with the Yankees that included a $900,000 signing bonus. Garland struck it rich in Cleveland; Grich, Baylor, and Rudi went to California; Tenace and Fingers signed with San Diego; Don Gullett went to the Yankees; Alexander and Campaneris signed with Texas; and the gold rush was on.

The trickle-down effect of free agency and the draft forced teams to consider locking up their most valuable players with long-term contracts before risking losing them to free agency. After earning $155,000 pitching for the Dodgers in 1976, ace right-hander Don Sutton signed a $1 million, four-year deal to remain in Los Angeles.

While the free agent draft ended in 1984, free agency was here to stay, forever changing the landscape of every element of professional baseball, from minor league operations to making trades.

"After Curt Flood, the next step in the process was when those fellows [Messersmith and McNally] worked without a contract," said Rick Wise. "That is what they did to move the issue forward to the next level. When I first broke into the majors in 1964, I didn't know about history. I didn't know about labor relations. I wanted to be a major league ballplayer since I was seven or eight. As an eighteen-year-old, I kept my eyes open and my mouth shut trying to absorb everything.

"It wasn't just Curt Flood and it stopped. It kept accelerating and accelerating. It finally went to arbitration and they said a one-year contract was a one-year contract. It took me fourteen years to become a free agent. Fred Lynn was a free agent right away. Wayne Garland signed for ten years. I wish free agency had happened earlier in my career."

While the reserve clause and the names Messersmith and McNally will go down in baseball history, it wasn't just free agency that has changed the game. Salary arbitration has also drastically changed the financial skyline of baseball.

Between 1976 and 1996, the average arbitration award rose from $68,000 to $2.3 million. The average salary in baseball in 1973 when the arbitration process was first introduced was $36,566. In 2005, the average salary was $2.63 million. The highest arbitration award to date went to Roger Clemens of the Houston Astros in 2005 for $18 million. That is the largest single-season salary for a pitcher in baseball history.

In his book *Pouring Six Beers at a Time and Other Stories from a Lifetime in Baseball*, Bill Giles explains the impact of arbitration on the salary structure of the game.

"Even before the Seitz decision created free agency, salary arbitration was agreed to by the owners and the Players Association," he wrote. "Arbitration's impact on Major League Baseball's salary structure is overshadowed by free agency, but it has been very significant. In fact, you will even hear some owners speak more ill of arbitration than of free agency. Salary arbitration is granted to a player after he has played three years in the major leagues, while free agency cannot occur until after six years. If a player and team cannot agree on a contract, the player can file for arbitration. Both the player and the team submit a figure and the arbitrator chooses one or the other. In virtually every case, even if the team's figure is chosen, the salary goes up, often dramatically. Most cases are settled before arbitration, as the team and player will often agree to a number between the two offers on the table rather than go through what is a fairly unpleasant process for everyone involved.

"Teams do not have to go to arbitration. Under the 2002–2006 labor agreement they can avoid it by not offering a contract to an arbitration-eligible player by December 20 of that year and trying to negotiate a better deal for the club—which occurs more frequently now than in the past. If the team can't get a deal done within a fixed window of opportunity, they can't re-sign the player until May 1 of the following year. This was the case with the Astros and Roger Clemens in 2006."

While all of this occurred too late for some of the players who toiled for years just on the cusp of the free agent/arbitration bonanza, the thought of losing a top performer for nothing more than a draft choice often causes teams to sign players to long-term contract extensions, or in many cases, trade the player while they can.

"Due to imposing free agency, trades are made," said Fred Claire. "A contract can be the trigger for the trade. That way you at least get something in return. In 2006 the Washington Nationals were very serious about trading Alfonso Soriano, not because they wanted to, but because they had to. If you look at the bigger trades, you can presume a reason for why the trades were made and it's usually because of contracts."

Contracts and the specter of losing a player who will become a free agent and getting nothing in return continue to be major concerns to organizations. And as long as contending teams are willing to give up talent to rent a player to get a chance to play in the postseason, the trade deadline will always be a fun and interesting time for baseball fans. But it makes trading for a player who may have little chance of being retained after the season a difficult decision with long-term implications for the franchise. Just how much of your future are you willing to mortgage for the chance to get into the postseason? And if you fail to make the playoffs and lose the player you have acquired for the short term, there is little left to show for the effort and the price your team has paid may come back to haunt you.

When a player is in what is called a contract year, the final year of an existing contract with free agency looming in his future, the dollars and cents don't always make sense.

"Since free agency and the increase of player compensation over the past thirty years, that is an element that has come into the exchange of players," said Pat Gillick. "The financial aspect has become almost bigger than the actual ability of the player. It's the length and the dollar amount of the contract which play a much more significant role in the contracts and trades now than they did in the past."

Two of the more interesting examples of renting players occurred in Houston, where the Astros went for the brass ring on more than one occasion. The Big Unit, Randy Johnson, has been one of baseball's best for nearly two decades. After breaking into the major leagues with Montreal, he was dealt to Seattle in the Mark Langston trade in 1989. What followed was an eight-year tenure with the Mariners that saw the powerful southpaw establish himself as one of the most consistent and overpowering pitchers in the game. He went 20-4 in 1997.

But with his contract up at the end of the 1998 season and with no chance to extend him beyond that season, the Seattle organization had little choice but to get what they could for their big left-hander. On July 31 of that year, Johnson, who had a 9-10 record with the Mariners, was traded to Houston in exchange for Freddy Garcia, Carlos Guillen, and a player to be named later, John Halama. All Johnson did was pitch in eleven regular season games for the Astros, sporting a spectacular 10-1 record with a 1.28 ERA. He allowed just fifty-seven hits in eighty-four innings and fanned 116 batters.

"He meant a lot to us in the second half of the season," said Tal Smith.

His overpowering performance helped the Astros win the Central Division title, only to lose to the New York Mets in the playoffs. Unable to sign Johnson, Houston watched helplessly as he signed a big-buck contract with the Arizona Diamondbacks.

Six years later, the Astros found themselves just out of contention for the playoffs again, needing a push to get them over the top. They had added pitchers Roger Clemens and Andy Pettitte in the off-season, but the lineup seemed to be missing a spark. Kansas City had an outstanding young outfielder named Carlos Beltran, who was entering the prime of his career. In his first five big-league seasons, Beltran hit .300 twice, hit at least twenty-two home runs four times, and drove in a hundred runs four times. He was twenty-seven years old, hitting .278 with fifteen home runs and fifty-one RBIs through sixty-nine games, and eligible to become a free agent at the end of the season.

A small-market team, the Royals had no chance to extend his contract beyond the season, so they entertained offers to acquire the talented budding star. Once again, it was Houston that stepped up to the plate and made a deal happen. On June 24 of 2004, a three-way deal was struck that saw Beltran sent to Houston, which sent John Buck and cash to Kansas City and Octavio Dotel to Oakland. The A's sent Mike Wood and Mark Teahen to the Royals.

"Obviously, it's bittersweet," Royals general manager Allard Baird said of the trade. "It was obvious we were not going to be able to sign Carlos. But I think we have helped this club and gotten some players that should have very productive Major League careers."

Beltran provided the offense that Houston needed, hitting .258 with twenty-three homers, driving in fifty-three runs, and helping the Astros leapfrog into the Wild Card. They beat the Braves in the playoffs before losing a heart-breaking extra-inning seventh game against the Cardinals to miss their first World Series. Beltran was unstoppable in the playoffs, setting a record with home runs in five consecutive games, tying Barry Bonds's record of eight post-season homers. But the Astros were unable to sign Beltran, who agreed to a seven-year $119 million contract with the New York Mets that winter. It was the tenth contract in the history of Major League Baseball worth more than $100 million.

"When I was with Kansas City I was always worried about being traded for five years," Beltran told ESPN. "When I was traded to Houston, it was not a good feeling. I didn't want to go through that anymore. I would not sign without a no-trade clause."

Andy Messersmith must have been smiling in his California home.

Certainly, the finances of baseball have changed dramatically over the last thirty years. Names such as Curt Flood, Andy Messersmith, and Dave McNally have been integral ingredients of the changes of Major League Baseball. For with the increased freedom of movement that baseball players have enjoyed, the financial aspects of the game have changed even more dramatically. While in the old days, clubs held all of the cards, in today's game, it is the players who have enjoyed most of the leverage.

Arbitration begat free agency, which has changed the way baseball teams build for the future. While there are no firm guidelines that hold true 100 percent of the time, some indications of the best way to approach free agent signings have been pretty consistent over the years.

In his article for the Baseball Analysts in 2006, "Long-Term Free Agent Contracts: A Historical Perspective," author David Regan did a study of any trends in the most effective ways to use free agency to help improve your club. The results are not all that surprising.

Regan wrote, "Hitters have historically been a better investment than their counterparts on the mound for teams looking to spend big money in free agency. There's not much risk in signing an under-30 superstar hitter to a long-term deal."

He then cites the names of successful position-player signings, including Alex Rodriguez, Manny Ramirez, Hideki Matsui, Cliff Floyd, Miguel Tejada, Vladimir Guerrero, Richie Sexson, Johnny Damon, Ellis Burks, Ray Durham, and Carlos Delgado. On the other hand, what have to be considered bad signings would include David Segui, Todd Hundley, Edgardo Alfonzo, Charles Johnson, Edgar Renteria, Roger Cedeno, David Bell, and Kaz Matsui. Of the players mentioned, the good certainly outweigh the bad.

Regan further concludes that homegrown is the way to go. Instead of overspending on guys who stand a great chance of underperforming once they sign, develop young, cheap pitching talent. As far as hurlers are concerned, the study suggests a path that not all clubs and general managers are disciplined enough to follow. Stay away from those long-term contracts for pitchers. Four words can sum up that strategy quite well: Mike Hampton, Carl Pavano.

"Contracts longer than three years for pitchers aren't a good idea," wrote Regan. "We've seen the rapid drop-off in years two and three of a deal and it likely won't get any better in year four."

Good pitching signings include Mike Mussina, Jason Isringhausen, Tom Glavine, Greg Maddux, Andy Pettitte, and Bartolo Colon. However, tens of millions of budget dollars have been pretty much wasted on the likes of Aaron Sele, Keith Foulke, Kevin Appier, Andy Ashby, Denny Neagle, Steve Karsay, Chan Ho Park, and the aforementioned Hampton and Pavano.

"It is unlikely that teams will continue to view the later years of a long-term deal as essentially 'sunk years,'" concluded Regan. "The Mets know that it's highly improbable that Billy Wagner will be worth eight figures in 2009, but it took adding the extra year to get the benefit of the 2006 and 2007 seasons. Unfortunately, for most teams, it's the type of deal that would bust budgets in and of itself, so the Wagners of the world will be reserved for the big-market teams only."

As has been the case for a number of years, the owners continue to be their own worst enemies, showing little or no discipline by paying average players exorbitant salaries, which continues to change the financial structure of the game. Aided by the new collective bargaining agreement and owners who spend recklessly, a cycle of mismanagement has resulted in marginal players earning huge amounts of money. Some owners refuse to act responsibly and ignore the new economics of the game.

Two owners whose names come to mind are Ted Turner of Atlanta and George Steinbrenner of the Yankees. While marquee players were deserving of bigger paydays that rewarded them for their excellence on the playing field, free agency saw many lesser players signing contracts for guaranteed money that was out of their league. It was Turner who opened the floodgates by giving a middle-of-the-road journeyman outfielder with a questionable work ethic, Claudell Washington, a contract he simply had not earned. While he had a smooth swing and great defensive skills, it was difficult for other owners to swallow the bitter pill of a slightly better than average player making marquee-player money. During his days with the Chicago White Sox, the Comiskey Park faithful became so frustrated with his lackadaisical style of play that they hung a sign in the stands that read "Washington Slept Here."

In fairness, Washington was what he was and had a long seventeen-year major league career. He can't be blamed for taking the money that was offered to him by the Braves. And in fairness to Turner and the Braves, Washington had his finest seasons in Atlanta, including 1984, when he hit .286 with a career-high seventeen home runs and sixty-one RBIs and played in the All-Star Game. But the lack of restraint exhibited by Turner and the Braves in signing a journeyman performer for a five-year deal worth $3.75 million resulted in shock waves throughout baseball.

Shortly after Washington signed his deal with Atlanta, Ruly Carpenter, whose family had owned the Philadelphia Phillies franchise for thirty-eight years, called a press conference during spring training of 1981. What was expected to be the announcement of a trade turned into the shocking statement by Carpenter that he was selling the team. Turner's signing of Claudell Washington was the straw that broke the camel's back.

"This is it," he said. "He [Washington] is coming off all those mediocre years. That's an unbelievable amount of money Ted Turner gave him. I'm out of here. When you start dealing with lawyers and agents instead of balls and strikes, I don't need it."

Carpenter was not the only owner-family that decided it was time to divest of its baseball franchise. In the ensuing years, the Wrigleys in Chicago, the Yawkeys in Boston, the Busches in St. Louis, and the Galbreaths in Pittsburgh all soon became former owners. As the players made more and more money, more and more of the old-fashioned family-owned teams became a thing of the past.

That questionable signing of Washington then led to more deserving players, such as Dave Winfield, getting even bigger contracts than they might have otherwise. It raised the bar. Winfield, a slugging outfielder with a cannon of a throwing arm, signed a ten-year contract to leave San Diego for the Yankees for $1.4 million per year. Unlike Washington, Winfield was a solid performer who blossomed into an even better player in New York in a career which was rewarded with induction to the Hall of Fame. During his tenure with the Yankees, he never hit below .262, smacked twenty-five or more home runs five times, and drove in at least one hundred runs six times. But at what cost?

Like any typical American business finding itself inundated with high wages and without control in dealing with its employees, Major League Baseball then made matters worse by attempting to bring salaries back down to a reasonable figure by agreeing to limit contracts—collusion.

In Article XVIII, Section H of the 1976 Major League Baseball Collective Bargaining Agreement, collusion is clearly defined. It states, "Players shall not act in concert with other Players and Clubs shall not act in concert with other Clubs." This agreement between the players and owners had its roots in the months before the 1966 season when outstanding Los Angeles Dodgers pitchers Sandy Koufax and Don Drysdale decided to act in concert by holding joint negotiations. The Dodgers could not sign one without the other. Both pitchers, who are now members of the Baseball Hall of Fame, held out for thirty-two days of spring training before agreeing to one-year deals. Koufax eventually signed for $125,000, while Drysdale penned a contract for $110,000, at the time the two largest contracts in baseball history.

In 1968, Marvin Miller agreed that players could not hold joint negotiations again as long as the owners agreed to the same principle. The previously cited article of the CBA was added to the agreement, which remained in effect into the mid-'70s, when it

Sandy Koufax could write his own ticket today.
Courtesy of the Los Angeles Dodgers.

seemed that something was amiss in Mudville. Shortly after being elected baseball commissioner in March of 1984, Peter Ueberroth devised a plan to help control player salaries and the bidding for free agent players. He suggested that beginning in 1985, teams should not make significant offers to free agent players if their current team wanted to keep them. While the plan did slow down the rapid growth in player contracts in 1985, 1986, and 1987, it was also illegal.

The collusion was not absolute, but it didn't take long to figure out what the owners were up to. In 1985 only four players changed teams, none of whom were wanted back by the teams they played for the previous year. Players such as Kirk Gibson, Tommy John, and Phil Niekro did not receive offers from other teams. Early the next year, the MLBPA filed its first collusion grievance.

During the off-season prior to the 1987 campaign, again only four free agents switched teams. One of the most obvious cases of collusion by the owners dealt with Chicago Cubs outfielder Andre Dawson, a former Rookie of the Year, perennial All-Star, Gold Glove Award winner, and one of the most feared hitters in the game. There was literally not a team in the league that could not have benefited from adding Dawson to their lineup. Yet, he received no free agent offers and eventually returned to the Cubs, signing a one-year contract for just $650,000, well below his market value.

Other players of note who had to return to their original clubs included Tim Raines, Jack Morris, Ron Guidry, Bob Boone, Rich Gedman, and Doyle Alexander. The players filed their second grievance seven months before arbitrator Thomas Roberts ruled that the owners had violated the basic agreement in their first grievance the year before.

In January of 1988, the players filed their third grievance, charging that the owners had created an information bank in which they shared information about what offers were being made to specific players, including Dennis Martinez, Jack Clark, and Paul Molitor.

A final settlement of $280 million was agreed upon for the owners to pay the players as a result of the three collusion cases.

Owners wanted it both ways. They had the desire to sign free agents, but only to the point where it did not hurt their team financially. Rather than practice restraint when offering contracts, they attempted to keep costs down by unfairly stacking the cards against the players. As Fay Vincent said to the owners, "The single biggest reality you guys have to face up to is collusion. You stole $280 million from the players, and the players are unified to a man around this issue because you got caught and many of you are still involved."

As Bill Giles added, "The level of trust by the players of the owners was severely, almost irrevocably damaged."

Arbitration, free agency, and the ever-increasing salary structure of Major League Baseball had put a strain on the way business was conducted. The powerful players' association had succeeded in increasing the power the players enjoyed. That, coupled with the loss of the reserve clause, changed the way that baseball was run and had a dramatic effect on how and why players were traded. Now, more than ever before, trades were being made for solely financial reasons.

Some teams were simply not capable of keeping star players whose contracts were coming to an end.

"But the biggest changes as far as trades are concerned have to do with the financial structure of the game," said Claire. "You can point to the Florida Marlins and how they made trades because of the financial structure of how the club saw itself and what it could afford."

It seems a universal point of agreement that free agency has drastically changed Major League Baseball in many ways. First and foremost, the economic aspect of the game has seen the players get a much bigger piece of the pie. As a result, gone are the days when a family of four can take in a ball game and consider it to be an inexpensive outing. Ticket prices have soared, as have the costs of food, drinks, novelties, and even parking. While these changes are obvious, the new financial aspect of the game, along with the tremendous increase in a player's control over his own destiny, has had a huge impact on how players are traded from one team to the next. Considering that a no-trade clause was what ultimately drove Andy Messersmith to play without a signed contract and take baseball to arbitration, the irony of this change in the game is hard to argue.

One of the most interesting deals since the advent of free agency involved the player universally known as "Junior," slugger Ken Griffey Jr. The son of the Cincinnati Reds Ken Griffey Sr., the younger Griffey has put up impressive power numbers in his stellar career. And there has never been even a hint of any sort of dishonesty on his part, such as steroid use. It is widely accepted that Junior is the real deal.

In his ten-year career with the Seattle Mariners, he hit 56 home runs two different times, as well as 49, 48, 45, and 40. In spite of numerous injuries that cost him considerable playing time, he entered the 2007 season with 563 career home runs. Had it not been for his ten stints on the disabled list in his eighteen big-league seasons, he most assuredly would have challenged Hank Aaron's all-time home run record. But his all-out effort in every aspect of the game, particularly in the outfield, has cost him countless games. Imagine the support that a healthy Junior would have garnered from fans all across the country if he were the player who challenged Aaron's homer mark. The only fault anyone has ever had with Ken Griffey Jr. is that if anything, he plays the game too hard, running with reckless abandon, diving for balls, and crashing into outfield fences. He is a throwback to the type of player who would probably pay to play.

After a number of seasons in which the Mariners contended for the playoffs and appeared in postseason play, the team slumped badly in 1998 and 1999. A devout family man, he moved his family from their Seattle home to the Orlando area and expressed the

desire to play for a contending team closer to them. He was earning $8.5 million with Seattle and the Mariners tried to extend his
contract by offering him a $148 million, eight-year deal to remain
with the team. But he informed chief executive officer Howard
Linder and general manager Pat Gillick that he did not care to
return in November of 1999.

"You should be able to anticipate and know who will sign a new
contract and who won't," said Gillick. "Some guys you have will
sign a new contract and others you have will be leaving. That was
a trade that Griffey requested. His parents lived in Cincinnati and
he wanted to be closer to them and end his career with the Reds.
It was more of a request by him to go back to the east. Cincinnati
would work for him and I think Atlanta would have worked as well.
Plus, he was a 10/5 man. When they get in that position, you have
your hands tied as they can veto, veto, veto any trade you want to
make, until they find it's where they want to go."

What followed was a very public negotiation that included discussions with four teams that Griffey said he would accept a trade
to, the Cincinnati Reds, New York Mets, Houston Astros, and
Atlanta Braves. But his heart was in Cincinnati, where he grew up
when his father was part of the Big Red Machine. In a day when
players give shallow comments about how their desires are not
strictly based on money, he was clearly willing to accept less money
to play in the Queen City.

At one point, he reportedly nixed a trade that would have sent
him to the Mets. Finally, after a long and involved process, Griffey
was traded to the Reds in exchange for Mike Cameron, Brett
Tomko, Antonio Perez, and Jack Meyer, ending three months of
almost constant negotiations. Following the trade, Griffey signed a
$112.5 million contract, which at the time was the biggest contract
in baseball history. Shockingly, it was widely accepted that Junior
could have earned much more money as a free agent. But in his
mind, he was returning home.

"Well, I'm finally home," Griffey said at a news conference following the trade. "This is something I dreamed about as a little kid, being back in my hometown where I watched so many great players."

Griffey went to the Reds, where he became the youngest player ever to hit 400 home runs, but injuries have halted what would have certainly been a full-scale assault on Henry Aaron's all-time home run mark. The Reds have never finished higher than second since the trade and have not played in the postseason since acquiring Griffey.

Seattle clinched a Wild Card on the final day of the 2000 season and swept the White Sox in the ALDS before losing to the Yankees in six games in the ALCS. In 2001, Seattle won the West with a 116-46 record and beat Cleveland in the ALDS, but lost once again to the Yankees in the ALCS.

An intriguing additional player to the business of baseball and negotiations is the player agent. This representative of the player is the point man for negotiations and many of the discussions with the organization. Agents are involved in many facets of the players' lives, from finding the best financial deal to helping them invest wisely with an eye toward the years following their playing career. Not only do agents help with contracts, but they also work to gain endorsement deals for their players and even act as public relations people.

"I think as far as the player is concerned, agents have had a very positive effect," said Jim Gott. "Before Curt Flood, you didn't really have a voice. All you could hang your hat on was your performance. An agent can give you a better understanding of what's going on with the team and your standing with the team that you as a player can't always get. Because of ESPN, all the plays of the day are out there immediately. The newspapers are now giving much more of an insider's view of the teams and with what's going on off the field. That's their angle. If you are one of the players who reads the papers and sees his name, it's easy to be confused about your role or spot on the team. You can't always just walk up to the general manager and ask about your situation. He's not always around the team and plus, your agent should already have a relationship there.

"A lot of guys are very uneducated business-wise and I'm one of them. Agents have connections for all sorts of things. I was lucky that my dad was a businessman and he helped me understand how important it is to be loyal to a guy who was doing a good job for you and looking out for your best interests."

But in some cases, the agents have become bigger than their clients and can have an adversarial relationship with team management representatives. Of course to be fair, there is no universal answer to the question of who made the relationship adversarial in the first place and who is just reacting in kind.

"The conversations with agents in those earlier days were, for the most part, civil and responsible with regard to the financial parameters we were working within," wrote John Schuerholz in *Built to Win*. "But as the salaries began to escalate dramatically, agents became more aggressive and some even arrogant.

"What I know from practical experience, from negotiating contracts, it is a system that completely works to the benefit of the player and agent. I am amused that some of them are regarded as super agents who are viewed as special and accomplished. Agents know—and those I talked to more often in the early days would acknowledge—the way you become a successful agent in this system is simply to learn how to say the word no and continue saying it.

"I don't have any desire any longer to deal with agents any more than necessary. I've determined that my having a slightly less-than-chilly relationship with them might be counterproductive. Agents are just doing their job. I understand that. And they are merely taking advantage of the flawed system that is in place.

"Agents play the system. Some have played the system so extensively they've gotten cocky and pompous simply because they represent these talented professional athletes."

Agents must also face the ultimate moral dilemma. What if your client has two offers, one from a team whose stadium fits his game, the other for more money from a team whose park could hurt his game? Consider an agent representing a pitcher who is considering a contract from the Colorado Rockies. The mile-high stadium eats pitchers up. But the agent gets paid a higher commission if the player makes more money.

"I know a lot of players who have gone ahead and made a decision that was not in the best interest of their career because of the money that was on the table," said Jim Gott. "The agent could be looking out for the biggest commission he can get and convince the player. Or the player can be anxious to get whatever he can as soon as he can because our window of opportunity to make this kind of money is small. I know when I played in Pittsburgh that Ray Miller used to say that these guys who would leave to go for more money didn't realize just how good they had it. Pittsburgh has a small-town feel to it and people love their sports stars. Bobby Bonilla went for huge dollars in New York and might have done better by staying with the Pirates."

The impact of agents on the game is not limited to helping players get a fair contract. Some of the more widely known, powerful agents represent numerous players whom they might be pitching to competing teams at the same time. Agents have played an important role as the game has changed.

"Their effect has been massive," said Bill Conlin. "I really think that agents have more power in the game than certain general managers. A guy like Scott Boros can actually influence pennant races with his clients. Thanks to the ties he had with the Boston Red Sox, he steered J. D. Drew to the Red Sox because of his relationship with Jason Varitek and Theo Epstein. When you get an agent with a stable of eight, ten, or fifteen high-profile players, he can orchestrate which clubs they will play for. That puts a whole lot of clubs without the financial wherewithal to overpay for these guys. And that's what teams do.

"When a team has a cap of $95 million and likes a certain player, the Yankees will outbid you every time. Bobby Bonilla was given a very generous offer by Philadelphia, but he and his agent used the Phillies to set the market. Bonilla had no intention whatsoever to play in Philadelphia. He signed with the Mets for just about what the Phillies offered. As soon as the number was established, the agent went to the Mets; they paid him a little more and he got to play where he wanted to all along."

The best possible scenario is when a player has an agent who is dedicated to him and his family, who is honest, liked, and respected by ownership, and who is looking out for the long-term interests of his clients. In spite of some of the horror stories and egomaniacal power brokers, there are a lot of agents who do a good job and are a positive part of the process.

"For most of my career, I had Jim Bronner," said Jim Gott. "He was awesome. My agents have been very important to me, making sure I had the best deal possible and even making sure that I had deferred money. I'm a bit of a nervous Nellie at times and to have someone hold my hand a little bit and make a call to the general manager just to let me know that I'm not on shaky ground and won't be going anywhere.

"The way the business is now, a player needs to have an agent. Are all agents good for the game? I don't think so. A lot of guys come in and try to make it big and compromise the integrity of their player or their position to try to make a name for themselves. It's a hard thing to become an agent. There is no rhyme or reason to it. If a guy gets a Derek Lowe, it significantly changes his ability to get other people. But if you're a small fish and nurturing a bunch of young guys, you still need that big fish to attract the other big fishes. You need to have four or five guys with big four- or five-year contracts.

"And for sure if you have some big significant players on one team, an agent can have a definite influence on the team."

8

BEING TRADED

The Player's Point of View

At some point in their working careers, many people have come across company owners who tell their employees that they consider them family. That they should go about their jobs as if they were partners with the owner of the company. That kind of loyalty to the company would always be rewarded and returned in kind by ownership to the hard-working employee-owners.

Sure. Of course, the feel-good atmosphere falls apart if the employee shows up late for work two days in a row. It's pretty much the same with baseball. A lot of lip service is given, but quite often, it is as sincere as a salesman's pitch.

"Today players are more transient than they used to be," said Tim McCarver. "The organizations used to preach that if you were a good boy they would take care of you. That was nonsense then and it is nonsense now. That blast of realism is more honest now than it was forty or fifty years ago. In the '60s and '70s, baseball had a paternalistic view of players. Everyone was treated more like family then and the first blast of realism hits you the first time you are traded. The first time a trade is made involving you, it's always difficult. It's very emotional because you've bought into this thing about them taking care of you and it is nonsense. They had no designs to do that and you get a little upset that you bought into it.

"The game is more like a business today. Trades are more or less accepted, although the first time is really difficult. You learn soon that this is a business we're in. You are signed to play baseball. There's no paternalism here. We're all grownups and need to approach it that way."

When a fan's favorite player is involved in a trade to a different city and team, it can be annoying and sad for the fan. But you can still root for a former member of your favorite ball club and criticize the team for the move every time the player in question wins a game or gets a hit. As a professional baseball player, however, it's your entire life that is thrown into a frenzy after being traded.

Most times, there is a spouse or girlfriend to consider. Older players have children in school, homes, friends, and traditions in the city in which they play. And then, with the suddenness of a walk-off home run, all that is history and you have three hours to catch a flight to meet your new team.

Rick Wise grew up in the Philadelphia Phillies organization. Signed out of high school, he broke into the majors in 1964 as an eighteen-year-old rookie. By 1971, he was the ace of the staff coming off a 17-14 season, including a no-hitter against the Cincinnati Reds in which he slugged two home runs in addition to hurling the no-no.

As the 1972 season approached, he had the audacity to ask for a significant raise and a salary hassle with the organization ensued. He had won in double figures in four of the previous five seasons and felt that a bigger payday was in order. So on February 25, 1972, Wise was shipped to the St. Louis Cardinals in exchange for another disgruntled pitcher who wanted a raise, southpaw Steve Carlton.

"It was crushing," said Wise. "Why was I traded? Looking back, I know it was about money. It was about the club's ability to control players. I was making only $25,000 after seven years in the big leagues. I won seventeen games, hit six home runs, and was an All-Star. And I pitched 272 innings. So I wanted to double my money, asking John Quinn for $50,000. He offered me a $10,000 raise.

"Being traded hurt. I didn't want to go to St. Louis. I had become the ace of the Phillies pitching staff at twenty-five. It hurt. We had bought our first house. My wife is from Pennsylvania and both my kids were born there.

"Lefty [Carlton] came in and did a tremendous job with the Phillies. He came in and went 27-10 for a team that won fifty-nine games. Carlton was having problems with Augie Busch. So we got traded and I got a little more than I asked for and Lefty got what he wanted from Philly. I don't have any bad feelings about the trade. Steve is a good friend of mine. But if I hadn't been good enough, the trade wouldn't have been made. The Cards didn't get hamburger in return. The trade was a case of both of the clubs saying that they're the bosses."

Coming off a 20-9 campaign with the St. Louis Cardinals, their left-handed hurler Steve Carlton also felt that a generous raise was in order. But the two general managers in question, John Quinn of the Phillies and Bing Devine of the Cardinals, felt differently. As Wise indicated, control was always an issue when management dealt with its players.

"Carlton had a high opinion of himself," Bing Devine wrote. "Rightly so, as it turned out. But Mr. Busch didn't like that. Here was a young pitcher who hadn't established himself. And Mr. Busch heard, without specific details, that this young pitcher was always difficult to sign.

"I'd like to think I could have kept Carlton around to see how great he would become. All I knew at the time was that he was a good young left-handed pitcher who had just turned 27, and I thought we should keep him. But his contract was up again that off season. Mr. Busch had a meeting with me and Dick Meyer, his right-hand man at Anheuser-Busch. And the team brain trust, if that's what you want to call it, decided that we ought to trade Carlton because we didn't have him signed and he wanted too much money.

"People forget now, but Rick Wise was a pretty good pitcher then. He was 17-14 the year before but his earned run average was 2.88, much better than Carlton's ERA in '71. And Wise had 155 strikeouts in 272 innings, almost as many as Carlton in '71. Wise went 16-16 his first year in St. Louis and 16-12 the next year, and then we shipped him to Boston.

"Getting rid of Carlton was not a deal that I initiated or tried to talk anybody into. It was just the relationship between Carlton and Mr. Busch."

That trade favored Philadelphia, particularly in the first year following the deal. Another lopsided trade, mentioned earlier, was when Lou Brock and others were traded for Ernie Broglio and others. One of the "other" players involved in that deal was young outfielder Doug Clemens, who put up big numbers in the minor leagues and actually became the Cubs' opening-day center fielder in 1965. While his success as an everyday player was short-lived, he did carve out a good career as a reserve and was an excellent pinch hitter. In fact, he set a major league record with three consecutive pinch hit doubles.

But no matter what stage your career is at, being traded uproots your life and career. He felt he would be a member of the St. Louis Cardinals for years to come. Such was not to be the case.

"I had put up some good numbers in the minor leagues and was considered a possible replacement for Stan Musial," Clemens said. "The reason I was included in the trade was that Larry Jackson, one of the Cubs pitchers, was a former teammate of mine who told John Holland, the Chicago GM, to make me part of the deal.

"I was devastated. I wanted to be a Cardinal. I had the opportunity to play with guys like Musial, Bill White, Bob Gibson, and Tim McCarver. And there I was going to Chicago. While we were not leading the league at the time in St. Louis, what it boiled down to was trying to be positive as a Cub and having an opportunity to play. It was quite traumatic to be traded. I had been there with St. Louis for four years and never even thought of a trade. And there I was going to the Cubbies with Broglio and Bobby Schantz for Brock and Paul Toth.

"Ironically, Paul Toth was an usher in my wedding. Then in '64 we're involved in the same trade. At the time I was shocked and hurt and sensitive to the issue that the Cards gave up on me. But I went to Chicago and had a good outlook on it."

It should also be noted that baseball owners have been the brunt of much criticism for the way in which they ran the game and totally controlled the players for so long. While the idea that a baseball team and its ownership are all part of a big, happy family has never been part of reality, there have been countless examples of ownership helping its players and showing them kindness and loyalty. Doug Clemens can attest to the human side of ownership, as well.

"When I played the major league minimum salary was $7,000," said Clemens. "I was just happy to be there. But the thing that really helped me was the baseball pension. I started collecting it at fifty-two.

"I had been with the Phillies for a couple of seasons, but was sent to Triple A San Diego in '68. I was twenty-two days shy of getting my pension. But the owner, Ruly Carpenter, told me to go to San Diego and help out some of the young players there and that he would bring me back at the end of the year so I could get the necessary time. And he did it."

The fact that players are traded, released, and sent back to the minor leagues by general managers and team executives does not mean that it is always a pleasant and easy move on their part. Players do have a degree of loyalty to their team and organization and, in fairness, many times members of management share loyalty and friendships with employees, which can often include players.

"You can develop a relationship with people associated with the club," said Tal Smith of the Houston Astros. "In many cases, you've known them and their families and it's particularly difficult when you raised the player in your organization. If a deal needs to be made, or as they get toward the end of their careers, there are real pangs of sentimentality. But you can't let that interfere with your decision. Trade discussions go on constantly, but because of talent or contracts, it's a very competitive business. You have to be objective. But you do have to remove any personal feelings you or the organization might have for a certain player. As a GM you take a different view.

"When I came back to the Astros in August of 1975, we were awful, a full 43.5 games out. We had to remake the club. I traded many of the veteran players I had known since the first day we signed them, like Roger Metzger, Larry Dierker, and Doug Rader. It was necessary to make these moves to remake the club.

"All I can say is that we went on to become a championship club four years later."

And sometimes it is the player who requests a trade. When that request is done privately, often the player can be sent to a better situation and the club is able to receive full value in return. But when that does not happen and the player goes public with his unhappiness, it becomes much more difficult for a club to make a deal because other general managers read the newspaper and might already by licking their chops in anticipation of making a trade.

"Bob Watson and I had a very close personal friendship when he played for the Astros," said Smith. "But he had some setbacks and didn't get the opportunity to play that he felt he deserved and asked to be traded. He and his wife, Carol, and I, are as close as a player and executive can be. He asked that we trade him and we did."

Of course, when a player makes trade demands publicly it's a different story. The parent club cannot shop a player quietly, or routinely ask waivers to see which teams may be interested.

Instead, a player making his demands public knowledge causes rival general managers to circle in the water like a shark sensing blood.

But the reality of a baseball trade in the years prior to Curt Flood's test of the reserve clause and the impact of Messersmith and McNally is that players had no say whatsoever in regard to where they would play. In fact, for some players even being told that they had been traded was asking too much of an organization. Larry Colton was once the player to be named later in a deal. It took him some time to find out about that distinction.

"As for being a player to be named later, which by the way, was the original title of *Bull Durham*, I didn't really feel too valued," Colton said. "In fact, the deal had actually been completed several weeks earlier and nobody from either organization had bothered to tell me. The Phillies had traded Johnny Callison and a player to be named later to the Cubs for Oscar Gamble and Dick Selma. It was sometime in December and I still hadn't received my contract from the Phillies, so I called the front office and got ahold of Dallas Green, who at the time was in charge of minor league development. He and I had been in spring training together a couple of years earlier and he had stayed in an apartment a few doors down from mine and we often rode to the park together.

"When I inquired about the contract, he said, 'Oh, didn't anybody tell you that you've been traded?' Nobody from the Phillies had called to say thanks or good riddance, but what bothered me even more was that the Cubs hadn't even called to welcome me to their organization. I had to contact them. That didn't bode well."

Sometimes a trade was welcomed and other times it was not. Relief pitcher Jack Baldschun experienced both sentiments in a period of just three days.

Baldschun had spent a number of very effective years coming out of the Philadelphia bullpen utilizing his out pitch, the screwball. On December 6, 1965, the Phillies traded him to the Baltimore Orioles in exchange for outfielder Jackie Brandt and left-handed reliever Darold Knowles. If he had to be traded anywhere, an American League team in general and Baltimore in particular was a good fit from Baldschun's perspective.

"Being traded is just hell," he said. "Number one, you don't ever figure you would be traded. When the trade came about, the Orioles called me on the phone and asked me if I'd like to be a Baltimore Oriole. I said I would. I was happy to be getting out of the National League because all of the hitters in that league knew about my screwball. I thought if I could get to the American League where they had not seen the screwball that I had another four or five years of good pitching. I was happy to go to Baltimore also because I was living in Philadelphia at the time and it was close by, just a ninety-mile drive or so.

"Three days later I got traded to Cincinnati. I was happy to go to Baltimore but I guess this thing with Cincinnati was in the making. The Reds wanted me back. I was glad to get away from there because they felt I was only so good. But I had done pretty well against them. I was not very happy. I wanted to be with Baltimore in the other league. Instead I was sent to the Reds with Milt Pappas and Dick Simpson as part of the Frank Robinson trade.

"You are bought, sold, and traded. It's just like slavery. But we were happy to be there making $7,000 a year. I'm so happy that I played when I did. In those days it was just baseball. It would be nice to be playing now because of the money, but millions and millions of dollars? It boggles the mind. You see Roger Clemens get all that money. Why? He should have retired years ago. And now he comes back in mid-season?

"It's a totally different game and it just boggles the mind. But I can't say I blame the players for getting the money. As has always been the case, I blame the owners."

It's hard not to get the impression that all trades leave the players involved feeling devastated and out of sorts. Fortunately, that is not the case. For every instance of a player seeing his professional and personal life set upside down, there is an example of a player who desperately needed a change of scenery. Or, a trade could be an example of a player finally getting that elusive opportunity to play on a regular basis. It's not all bad; in fact, sometimes a trade is a breath of fresh air in a player's career that enables him to reach his full potential.

Such was the case with pitcher Jim Gott, whose career in the St. Louis Cardinals organization had finally hit a brick wall in 1981 after five minor league seasons. Following a 5-9 season with Arkansas of the Texas League, he was a Rule 5 draft choice of the Toronto Blue Jays.

"My experience is that I was in the Cardinals organization and had not had very good statistics in the minor leagues," Gott said. "So I went to winter ball and did really well when I got away from the structure of the Cardinals organization. I was left off the roster in the winter of '81 and got picked up by the Toronto Blue Jays and had the opportunity to make the team in spring training, which I did. Going from one team to another could not have possibly happened at a better time for me.

"The big thing with the Blue Jays was that while the Cardinals nurtured me and knew my background, to the Blue Jays I was new with a fresh perspective. They didn't feel they needed to change my delivery or my pitches. They just wanted to give me confidence and the opportunity to pitch in the big leagues. I went from being at least two years away from the majors in the Cards organization to being on the major league roster in Toronto."

The six-foot-four-inch right-hander responded with three good, albeit inconsistent seasons with Toronto, as his 21-30 record would indicate. But another move was on Jim Gott's horizon and this too was a positive change.

"When I was with the Blue Jays, I had the opportunity to close a little bit in 1984. I liked it but was a little immature. I was sent to the Giants (along with Augie Schmidt and Jack McKnight), another last-place team, in exchange for Gary Lavelle. I had the opportunity to start over there and have to admit that I sure loved

A change of scenery changed Jim Gott's career.
Courtesy of the Los Angeles Dodgers.

hitting, which I could do in the National League. It was another fresh start and that's what all my moves were.

"My first three years in the majors I had been very inconsistent. I was excited to be with the Giants because I had spring training on the West Coast for the first time and my family was there. But I hurt myself in 1986 and missed almost the whole season. The Giants made a lot of changes and Al Rosen came in with Roger

Craig. I pitched really well in spring training of '87 and made the team, but didn't really have a spot, basically being the eleventh pitcher on a ten-man staff. The next thing I knew, they put me in a deal to Pittsburgh with Mackey Sasser for Don Robinson. But on my birthday, August 3, 1987, I cleared waivers and went from the Giants to the Pirates. It was the best thing in the world for me.

"I was on a young Pirate team led by Jim Leyland and Syd Thrift, two demanding but nurturing people. My teammates were people like Barry Bonds, Jose Lind, and Doug Drabek. I was supposed to be a starter, but they needed someone in the bullpen and I had a real positive attitude and got saves in my first two opportunities. But I failed my third time out and was walking into the clubhouse with my head down. Leyland and Ray Miller, our pitching coach, saw me walk by when Leyland pushed me up against the wall and put his finger in my face and told me, 'Listen, we don't give up on anyone around here. You be ready tomorrow.' That was just what I needed.

"Every single move in my career was positive for my career and my life. I became a free agent after the '89 season when the Pirates didn't think I could make it back from an injury and I got an opportunity to pitch for the Dodgers for six more seasons in the big leagues."

9

HIGHWAY ROBBERY

Picking the Pocket of Another Team

No matter what the typical fan might think, when a trade is made between two baseball teams, one general manager is not trying to pick the pocket of his counterpart and get the better of him. In baseball's best-case scenario, trades work out for both teams. The players they acquire play well, fitting in their new circumstances perfectly. And if a player needs a change of scenery, the new mailing address makes him play with the energy and vigor of a rookie who has the experience to avoid rookie mistakes.

Of course, the reality is that while trades have often helped both teams, there have also been quite a few cases where one team smells the roses, while the other team smells the manure.

The Brock-for-Broglio deal has been discussed for years, as well as earlier in this book. There is no need to go back there again. But there have been countless other examples of deals that just didn't work out for both teams; trades that benefited one team and one team only. But again, that is never really the desire of GMs. They are just trying to improve their team, use an excess they might have, rid the team of a troublemaker, or get something in return for a player about to become a free agent.

The Babe Ruth sale was probably the biggest bad deal in the history of the game. Brock-for-Broglio is also right up there. But there are numerous other examples of trades that leave you shaking your head, wondering if the general manager in question knew what he was doing. He did. But the rest of us have the benefit of 20/20 hindsight, which isn't always kind or fair.

But remember the words of Bing Devine: "If you never have the guts to do anything, you'll never get lucky. You'll never give yourself the chance to be lucky."

When a trade is made, both teams are taking a chance. Sometimes, however, only one team gets lucky. Here are some examples of such occurrences.

CHRISTY MATHEWSON FOR AMOS RUSIE

In the last decade of the nineteenth century, Amos Rusie was one of the best pitchers in baseball. He had a blinding fastball that played a part in the pitcher's mound being moved from fifty feet from home plate to sixty feet and six inches when he seriously injured a player, Hughie Jennings, with one of his pitches. As John McGraw said of Rusie's heater, "You can't hit what you can't see."

After breaking into the major leagues with Indianapolis in 1889, he signed with the New York Giants after the Indianapolis team folded and immediately made an impact as a nineteen-year-old by winning twenty-nine games in 1890, although he lost thirty-four that season. What followed was a stretch of eight consecutive seasons in which he won at least twenty games and four straight years when he won at least thirty.

But he sat out the 1896 season in a contract dispute with the Giants, whose owner, Andrew Freedman, had often fined Rusie for missing curfew and partying with teammates and friends long into the evening. Fearful that a court case would damage the reserve clause, owners pooled their money to settle Rusie's court case and give him the raise he desired. He came back to pitch again in 1897, not missing a beat with a 28-10 record.

But the following season, en route to a 20-11 record, Rusie damaged the pitching arm that earned him the nickname "The Hoosier Thunderbolt." He sat out the '99 season in another salary dispute and could not agree on a contract in 1900.

Giants owner Freedman was fully aware that Rusie's arm was shot, but he was involved in negotiations to sell a controlling interest in the Giants to Reds owner John Brush, who desired to be involved in the New York market. But Brush insisted that the only way he would make the trade was if he were able to bring one of the Reds' top young pitching prospects, Christy Mathewson, with him. So a few weeks before the sale of controlling interest in the team was finalized, the trade of the shot pitcher Rusie for Mathewson was made.

With Cincinnati, Rusie pitched in just three games with an 0-1 record and an ERA of 8.59. To illustrate just how shot the former flamethrower was by the time he turned thirty years of age, in

The trade between Amos Rusie and Christy Mathewson was as one-way as a trade gets.
National Baseball Hall of Fame Library, Cooperstown, NY.

twenty-two innings with the Reds he surrendered forty-three hits and twenty-one earned runs.

Meantime, the nineteen-year-old Mathewson broke in with an 0-3 record in six games with the Giants before winning twenty in 1901. What followed was an illustrious career that saw him amass 373 victories against just 188 losses and an incredible career ERA of 2.13. He won at least twenty games for twelve consecutive years, won at least thirty games four times, and pitched shutouts in eighty of his career victories. In 1908, he had his best season, with a 37-11 record with a 1.43 ERA. But Mathewson followed up that campaign in 1909 by going 25-6 with a microscopic 1.14 ERA.

Unlike Rusie, who was known for his off-the-field antics, Mathewson was not the typical hard-living, hard-drinking ballplayer of the day. He attended Bucknell University, where he was a member of the glee club as well as the literary society. He also wrote a series of children's books.

Grantland Rice said of Mathewson, "Christy Mathewson brought something to baseball no one else had ever given the game. He handed the game a certain touch of class, an indefinable lift in culture, brains, and personality."

At the end of his seventeen-year career, Mathewson finished his playing days as a member of the Reds, who acquired him along with Bill McKechnie and Edd Roush in exchange for Buck Herzog and Red Killefer. In his lone appearance with the Reds, his final appearance in the major leagues, Mathewson earned a win.

He joined Babe Ruth, Honus Wagner, Ty Cobb, and Walter Johnson in the first class of Hall of Fame inductees in 1936. Amos Rusie was also elected into the Hall of Fame in 1977.

JOHN SMOLTZ FOR DOYLE ALEXANDER

In August of 1987, Detroit sent young pitching prospect John Smoltz to the Atlanta Braves in exchange for veteran pitcher Doyle

Alexander. At first, it appeared that the Tigers got the best of the deal. All the crafty Alexander did was go 9-0 for Detroit with a stellar ERA of 1.53 in eleven starts. He gave the Tigers the boost they needed to win the American League East division crown. Although they lost the ALCS in five games to the Minnesota Twins, with Alexander going 0-2, the trade was still considered a major coup for Detroit.

Alexander followed up with another good season in 1988, going 14-11 and pitching 229 innings. The Tigers finished a mere game behind the division-winning Boston Red Sox. But Alexander slipped to a 6-18 record for a Tiger team in 1998 that slipped even further, finishing in last place in the AL East, thirty games behind Toronto and forty-four games under .500. After the season, Alexander announced his retirement at the age of thirty-nine. He finished his nineteen-year career with a 194-174 record with a 3.76 ERA.

Prior to being traded, Smoltz had a 4-10 record with Glens Falls of the Eastern League. He then was assigned to the Atlanta Triple A team in Richmond, where he went 0-1 in three games. In 1988, Smoltz showed dramatic improvement, as his 10-5 record with Richmond with a 2.79 ERA in twenty games would indicate. He was recalled to Atlanta and pitched in twelve games for the Braves, garnering a less-than-impressive 2-7 record with an inflated 5.48 ERA.

A big leaguer for good in 1989, Smoltz began a streak of five seasons in which he won fifteen games twice, fourteen games twice, and twelve games once. His finest season was 1996, when he went 24-8, leading the league in wins, innings pitched, winning percentage, and strikeouts. But after being slowed down by arm problems, Smoltz became one of the best closers in the game, raking up 154 saves over a four-year period before returning to the starting rotation.

With more than 200 career wins to go along with the 154 saves, it seems a certainty that five years after his playing career is completed, John Smoltz will join his Atlanta Braves pitching partners for so many seasons, Tom Glavine and Greg Maddux, in baseball's Hall of Fame.

LARRY BOWA AND RYNE SANDBERG FOR IVAN DEJESUS

Hindsight is certainly always 20/20, but just the thought of making this deal from the Philadelphia Phillies' perspective seems absurd. Which was worse, the trade that sent future Hall of Famer Ryne Sandberg to the Cubs, or the trade that sent future Hall of Famer Ferguson Jenkins to the Cubs? That's a tough one to answer.

Shortstop Larry Bowa had enjoyed a fine career with the Phillies. He was a gutsy, vocal leader on the team who could motivate as well as annoy. Because Bowa felt that Bill Giles, one of the new owners, reneged on a promise made to him by former owner Ruly Carpenter about a new contract, Bowa and Giles were at odds during the 1981 season. When former Phillies manager Dallas Green and his coach, Lee Elia, left the Phillies for the Cubs, it seemed only natural that Chicago could be a destination for Bowa should he leave the Phillies.

On January 27, 1982, the Phillies traded Bowa and young infielder Ryne Sandberg to the Cubs in exchange for their shortstop Ivan DeJesus. It was a stopgap measure to get the aging Bowa out of town and bring in a fine defensive shortstop in DeJesus to replace him. But it seems that the idea to include the future Hall of Famer, Sandberg, in the deal may have actually come from Larry Bowa.

Dallas Green named Lee Elia the Cubs manager and the former Phillies coach was playing golf with Bowa one day. It was Bowa who suggested to Elia that if they trade for him, Chicago should insist that Sandberg be part of the deal.

"I told him [Elia] that I knew his [Sandberg's] work habits at that time were considered lazy," Bowa said in *Larry Bowa: I Still Hate to Lose*. "Very, very low key. But I'm telling you, he's going to be a player.

"So they finally put the deal together. The Chicago writers call me up. And I didn't know the final trade yet. So I asked, 'Who's the guy they threw in?' When they said Sandberg, I told them, 'Well then, I was the guy they threw in because Sandberg is going to be a great player.'

"Of course, I was proven right on that one. He turned out to be a spectacular second baseman."

Actually, DeJesus was a very serviceable shortstop. After breaking in with the Dodgers organization, he was dealt to the Cubs, where he became a regular in 1977. In five seasons with Chicago, DeJesus hit as high as .283 and as low as .194 in 1981, the year before he was traded to the Phillies. But he was considered a fine fielder who might actually be an upgrade from Bowa, at that point in his career.

Sandberg was thought of as a good prospect in Philadelphia, but following a solid season with Double A Reading in 1980 when he hit .310, the following year at Triple A Oklahoma City, he hit a solid .293. A late-season call-up to the Phillies saw him appear in just thirteen games with one hit in six at bats.

"When the Phillies first called Sandberg up from the minors, he actually played center field," said Bill Conlin. "At that time you had Larry Bowa at shortstop, the greatest third baseman of all time [Mike Schmidt], and Manny Trillo at second base. There was no place to immediately slot him in and they didn't think he would be a real good center fielder. Once again, they failed to have a plan in place for a player who had obvious offensive skills. Hughie Alexander, who was still with the Phillies, admitted to me that he wanted Dallas to get a real good player in addition to Bowa. Hughie said that he liked Sandberg but that he was blocked because he didn't have a position with the Phillies."

The rest is history.

JEFF BAGWELL FOR LARRY ANDERSEN

During his seventeen-year major league career, Larry Andersen was a serviceable big-league hurler. He amassed a 40-39 won/lost record with forty-nine saves and an ERA of 3.15. He started just one game. While he wasn't a closer, Andersen was a setup guy who would come in to a tie game or would be charged with protecting a lead in order to get to the closer at the back of the bullpen.

He didn't blow hitters away with a blazing fastball. What he did was tantalize batters with his slider. The pitch seemed destined to be on the outer half of the strike zone, teasing the hitter with what seemed to be a line-drive hit just waiting to happen. But as they began their swing at the pitch, it would break away, just out of their reach. And with each ensuing slider, he'd make the hitter look worse and worse.

In 1990, Boston needed a setup guy who could also close in their pennant drive. So they dealt Jeff Bagwell, a twenty-two-year-old third baseman who had just completed his third minor league season with the Sox Double A farm club in New Britain, where he had his career-best batting average of .333 with four home runs and sixty-one RBIs.

Andersen helped Boston into the playoffs, pitching in just fifteen games with a 1.23 ERA. But the veteran converted on just one of four save opportunities and the Red Sox won the division before falling to Oakland in four straight games in the ALCS. After negotiating to stay in Boston, he eventually signed with the San Diego Padres, where he played for two years before closing out his career with the Phillies in 1993 and '94.

Bagwell, along with Craig Biggio, became Houston's favorite son over a fifteen-year period in which they led the Astros' powerful offense. Bagwell became a star in Houston, finishing his career with a .297 average, with 449 home runs and 1,529 RBIs. He hit at least thirty home runs and drove in at least one hundred runs for six consecutive seasons from 1996 to 2001. He appears to be a lead-pipe cinch to be elected to baseball's Hall of Fame.

"I'm glad that I was a part of the Bagwell plot to doom the Bosox," Andersen said in an interview with the website Astros Daily. "At least that's the way most people look at it in retrospect. Most people will say that I helped them win the division, and that I believe is true. What they won't admit is that they would have been in an uproar if they had traded [Scott] Cooper. He was ahead of Bagwell and maybe a more thought-of prospect. Bagwell led the league in average [AA] but had only four homers. Who knew he was gonna put on 30-40 pounds and become a tremendous run producer?

"Nevertheless, I have no regrets and even have a lot of fun with it. My agents, Alan and Randy Hendricks, even made a proposal to the Sox for a two-year deal that they rejected. That was one thing that made the trade so bad also. I was only there for one month and they didn't get anything in return for me as I was declared a 'new look' free agent and signed with San Diego. Boston actually came back and made a significantly better offer than the one we proposed to them that was turned down. It was just one of those things that has haunted Boston for decades. Bagwell also seems to have fun with it. In fact he once introduced me to Mike Hampton and said 'Hampy, that's the guy I made famous,' as he pointed to me. It makes people who don't know any different think I was a better player than I was. Not many people can say they got traded one-for-one with somebody as good as he is. Plus, I know I'll be in the news all around the country, articles, newscasts, and ESPN every July. Would I be that famous if I got traded for Scott Cooper? Or is it infamous?"

MARK MCGWIRE FOR T. J. MATTHEWS, ERIC LUDWICK, AND BLAKE STEIN

The Oakland Athletics are known for making the most out of being a small-market team that cannot normally bid on high-priced superstars. It makes it especially difficult when a homegrown talent has a salary structure that has outgrown the A's ability to pay him. Such was the case with slugging first baseman Mark McGwire in 1997. Coming off an outstanding season in 1996, hitting .312 with fifty-two home runs and 113 RBIs, there was very little chance that he would re-sign with Oakland when his contract expired at the end of the '97 campaign.

Though he was hitting .284 with thirty-four homers and eighty-one RBIs at the end of July, on the thirty-first of that month Oakland dealt their powerful slugger to the St. Louis Cardinals for a trio of right-handed pitchers, T. J. Matthews, Eric Ludwick, and Blake Stein. McGwire became a household name because of his battle with the Cubs' Sammy Sosa to break Roger Maris's all-time single-season home run record of sixty-one in 1998. The best that could be said about the three right-handed pitchers the A's got in return was that they were all tall.

Ludwick, six foot five, was 0-1 with St. Louis in five games with a 9.45 ERA prior to the trade. He pitched in four games for the A's, posting a 1-4 record with an 8.25 ERA. Following the season, he was dealt to Florida in exchange for Kurt Abbot.

Stein, who stood at six foot seven, came up to Oakland in 1998 and went 5-9 in twenty-four games with a 6.37 ERA. He was traded the following season with Jeff D'Amico and Brad Rigby to Kansas City for pitcher Kevin Appier.

Matthews, only six foot two, was the best pitcher acquired in the trade. After a 4-4 start with the Cardinals, he boasted a 6-2 mark in twenty-four games with a 4.40 ERA for Oakland. He spent parts of four seasons with the A's and his eight-year career mark was 32-26. But the real story of this trade was Mark McGwire.

He finished his sixteen-year career in 2001 with a lifetime .263 batting average, but he slugged 583 home runs and drove in 1,414. He and his friend Sosa brought millions of fans back to baseball with their torrid 1998 season that saw McGwire hit 70 home runs and knock in 147 runs for the Cardinals.

During his career, he hit at least 30 home runs eleven times, including 49 in 1987, 42 in 1992, 52 in 1996, 58 in 1997, the afore-mentioned 70 in 1998, and 65 in 1999. Even though he hit 58 ding-ers in 1997, he didn't lead either league as he was traded in mid-season.

Much controversy has ensued over the years because of alleged steroid use by numerous big-league players. It has never been proved that McGwire ever used an illegal performance-enhancing drug. In fact, he admitted to using Androstenedione, which was a legal over-the-counter diet supplement.

No matter how much controversy might arise over McGwire's career, there can be no doubting his excellent power numbers. It might also be noted that he hit a rookie-record forty-nine in 1987, long before there was any hint of possible steroid use.

DEREK LOWE AND JASON VARITEK FOR HEATHCLIFF SLOCUMB

It's doubtful that many Boston Red Sox fans felt that when the Bosox acquired Derek Lowe and Jason Varitek in a 1997 trade with Seattle for slumping reliever Heathcliff Slocomb that they had put two key ingredients to their World Series championship team of 2004 in place. But that is just what happened.

Lowe was struggling with a 2-4 record in twelve games with Seattle in his rookie campaign when dealt to Boston. From 1998 through 2001, he showed promise as a reliever with an 18-26 record with eighty-one saves out of the pen, including forty-two in 2000. But the following July, the Red Sox acquired closer Ugueth Urbina, who moved into the closer's role. Urbina threw harder than Lowe, a more typical closer.

In 2002, Lowe became a full-time starter, posting a 21-8 record and an excellent 2.58 ERA. He also tossed a no-hitter against Tampa Bay on April 27, the first Fenway Park hitless game since Bosox hurler Dave Morehead did the trick in 1965. He was 17-7 the following year and boasted a 14-12 mark in the magical 2004 season. Lowe's big-game value rose in the playoffs as he became the first pitcher in baseball history to win the final game of three postseason series, beating Anaheim, the Yankees, and St. Louis. His success enabled him to cash in on a big-money free agent deal with the Los Angeles Dodgers.

Varitek became a team leader and the regular catcher in 1999, hitting .269 with twenty home runs and seventy-six RBIs. A solid and dependable backstop, he had another outstanding season in 2003, hitting .273 with twenty-five homers, driving in eighty-five runs. In 2004, he hit a career-high .296 with eighteen dingers and seventy-three RBIs.

It was ironic that Varitek became such a standout in Boston, as he played two summers for the Hyannis Mets of the Cape Cod league, winning the league's Most Valuable Player award and leading the league with a .371 average in 1993.

In fairness to Slocomb, the trade seemed like a good one for the Mariners, who were desperate for help out of the bullpen. A journeyman reliever, Slocomb had pitched for the Cubs and Cleveland before having his breakout season with the Phillies in 1994, appearing in fifty-one games with a 5-1 record and a stingy 2.86 ERA. Moving into the closer's role the following season, he had a 5-6 record with thirty-two saves and a 2.89 ERA in sixty-one games.

Acquired by the Red Sox that winter, he went 5-5 with Boston in 1996 with thirty-one saves and a 3.02 ERA. But he made himself expendable the following season, getting off to an 0-5 start with seventeen saves and a high ERA of 5.79. Following the trade to Seattle, his troubles continued as he went 0-4. In parts of two seasons with the Mariners, he appeared in ninety-four games with a 2-9 record and just thirteen saves.

In 1999, Slocomb pitched well in forty games with St. Louis with a 3-2 record and a 2.36 ERA, but he was no longer considered a closer out of the pen, converting on one of two save opportunities. In 2000, he was not as effective, sporting a 2-3 record but a high ERA of 5.44 before finishing his major league career with twenty-two games later that season with San Diego.

FRANK ROBINSON FOR MILT PAPPAS, DICK SIMPSON, AND JACK BALDSCHUN

As bad baseball trades go, this one is difficult to top. Frank Robinson began his big-league career in Cincinnati in 1956, hitting .290 with thirty-eight home runs and eighty-three RBIs, good enough to earn him Rookie of the Year honors. Over the decade he spent with the Reds, all Robinson did was hit .300 five times, smack at least thirty home runs seven times, never hit below twenty-one, and drive in at least a hundred runs four times. Even in 1965, in what was his final year in Cincinnati, he hit .296 with thirty-three homers and 113 RBIs.

Throughout his career, Frank Robinson earned the type of statistics that could lead you to believe that he had Triple Crown potential, leading his league in average, home runs, and RBIs. That is, of course, unless you were Reds' president Bill DeWitt, or among the throngs of Cincinnati fans who continuously, mercilessly booed and hounded Frank Robinson. He was not a troublemaker, not a hotdog, and not a malingerer. He was a clutch, hardnosed player and competitor.

According to *The History of the Reds: 1960–1969*, "Frank Robinson had a moderately turbulent relationship with Cincinnati fans. At the time he was the first black star player for the Reds. It seemed no matter how well Robinson played, it was never good enough. During the 1965 season, Reds fans booed him regularly. During a game in Cincinnati, the booing became so bad that Reds Manager Dick Sisler made an announcement on the PA to Reds fans to lay off Robinson. Reds fans persisted and regularly wrote to Reds management demanding that he be traded. DeWitt did exactly that and traded him to the Baltimore Orioles. Frank Robinson proceeded to win the American League MVP, the Triple Crown and guided the Orioles to their first World Series championship in 1966. Milt Pappas, Jack Baldschun and Dick Simpson never panned out for the Reds."

That may be an understatement. The trade of Robinson for Pappas, Baldschun, and Simpson is such a glaring example of a bad trade that it is even immortalized in the baseball movie *Bull Durham*, when Annie Savoy states, "Bad trades are a part of baseball. I mean who can forget Milt Pappas for Frank Robinson, for gosh sakes?"

Who indeed? In fairness, Milt Pappas was a very good pitcher who compiled a 209-164 record during his seventeen-year career. Born Milton Stergios Papasterigos, Pappas broke into the Show as an eighteen-year-old in 1957, appearing in four games. The following season he went 10-10 and the next went 15-9. During his eight full seasons in Baltimore, he was 110-74, never won fewer than ten games, pitched at least 200 innings six times, and never surrendered more hits than innings pitched.

Baldschun and Simpson arrived in Cincinnati via teams with whom they never appeared in a game. Simpson was sent to Baltimore from the California Angels that winter in exchange for Norm Siebern. Unlike Baldschun, the young outfielder had little big-league experience prior to the trade.

Baldschun was a fine reliever whose best pitch was a screwball. He had a string of five successful seasons out of the bullpen for the Philadelphia Phillies, sporting a 39-34 record with fifty-nine saves. After the 1965 season, the Phillies dealt him to Baltimore in exchange for outfielder Jackie Brandt and pitcher Darold Knowles, only to be packaged as part of the deal for Frank Robinson just three days later.

"I was so happy to be an Oriole," said Jack Baldschun. "Then just a couple of days later I was a Red. I was not glad to be included on the bottom end of the deal that would go down as one of the worst trades in baseball. But at least my name is still out there. I thought I was one of the better relief pitchers in baseball at the time."

Frank Robinson had the season of seasons in 1966 with the Orioles, hitting .316 with a career-high forty-nine home runs and 122 RBIs. He won the Triple Crown, became the first person to win the MVP award in both leagues, and was the All-Star and World Series MVP. Robinson, who played baseball in high school with Curt Flood and Vada Pinson as well as high school basketball with Bill Russell, had six strong seasons with Baltimore. He also had productive seasons with the Los Angeles Dodgers and California Angels before finishing his Hall of Fame playing career with the Cleveland Indians, who made him the first black manager in Major League Baseball.

Dick Simpson played in ninety-two games for Cincinnati in 1966, hitting just .238 with four home runs and fourteen RBIs. The following season he saw action in just forty-four games and was dispatched following the season to St. Louis in exchange for slugging outfielder Alex Johnson. At the age of twenty-five, Simpson was gone from the majors for good after the 1969 season with a career .207 batting average.

Baldschun fared a little better. Beset by a pair of catchers, Johnny Edwards and Jim Coker, who had difficulty catching and utilizing his baffling screwball, Baldschun slumped to a 1-5 record in 1966 with no saves. His ERA that season was 5.49, considerably higher than his previous highest mark of 3.88. Appearing in just nine games the following season, he was released.

He did work his way back to the major leagues with San Diego in 1969 and '70, where he enjoyed an 8-2 record. But neither Pappas, Simpson, or Baldschun enjoyed anywhere near the success of Frank Robinson, who turned out to be anything but an old thirty-year-old. The slugging outfielder played a total of twenty-one major league seasons and was productive right to the end of his playing career. He finished with a .294 batting average, with 586 home runs, fourth on the all-time list. He also drove in 1,829 runs, which is tenth best on baseball's all-time list.

10

ODD DEALS IN
BASEBALL HISTORY

"Balls!" said the Queen. "Give me twelve dozen and I'll give you Tim Fortugno!"

Well, not exactly. But that takeoff on the old joke with the Queen exclaiming, "Balls, if I had two I'd be King," gives a glimpse into some of the weirdest types of player transactions ever concocted.

Tim Fortugno was a journeyman left-handed pitcher who toiled for fifteen professional teams during a career that saw him pitch in seventy-six major league games, garnering a 3-4 record. Not unlike most players, he was involved in trades and transactions during his career, some that could be classified as typical trades. But another deal that he was involved in has to be one of the most unusual in the history of America's Game.

In 1987, Fortugno was sent from the Seattle Mariners along with outfielder Phil Bradley to the Philadelphia Phillies in exchange for Glenn Wilson, Dave Brundage, and Mike Jackson. He was also part of another major trade eight years later when he was sent, along with Jim Abbott from the Chicago White Sox, to the California Angels in exchange for McKay Christensen, John Snyder, Andrew Lorraine, and Billy Simas.

Pretty normal, everyday baseball stuff. But between those two transactions, Fortugno was part of one of the strangest deals in the history of baseball. On May 5, 1989, he was traded by the Reno Silver Sox to the Milwaukee Brewers organization in exchange for $2,500 and twelve dozen baseballs.

HOPE IT WASN'T A LEISURE SUIT

If misery likes company, Tim Fortugno will never be alone. In the history of baseball, there are countless examples of absolutely crazy trades. For instance, even the most pedestrian baseball fan is familiar with Cy Young, who amassed 511 victories in his major league career. But in 1890, the future Hall of Famer was traded by the minor league team he was playing for in Canton to the major league Cleveland club for $250 and a suit of clothes.

A PITCHER FOR A FENCE

Another Hall of Fame pitcher, Lefty Grove, had his contract acquired by the Philadelphia Athletics in 1925 for a record price at the time—$100,600. But only five years before, while pitching for the minor league Martinsburg Mountaineers, he was traded to the Baltimore Orioles in exchange for an outfield fence. A storm had destroyed the fence in June of that year and the O's agreed to pay for the replacement in exchange for one of the greatest pitchers of all time.

TRADED FOR OYSTERS? OH, SHUCKS

Oyster Joe Martina was the second winningest pitcher in the history of the minor leagues with 349 wins, second only to Bill

Thomas, who earned 383 wins. But unlike Thomas, Martina pitched one season in the major leagues in 1924 with the world champion Washington Senators, sporting a 6-8 record in thirty-four games. He also pitched a scoreless inning in the World Series. But three years earlier, Martina earned his Oyster Joe moniker after he was dealt by Dallas to New Orleans in exchange for two barrels of oysters.

THE STRANGE TRADE OF CATFISH KENNY

Fans of *The David Letterman Show* or *Good Morning America* might remember the strange journey of Catfish Kenny Krahenbuhl. A ninth-round draft choice of the Chicago Cubs, Krahenbuhl was an unlikely guest on such shows, considering that his pitching career had been pretty much stalled by arm injuries that left him toiling in Oxnard, California, for the Pacific Suns Independent League team. On July 22, 1998, the Suns traded their pitcher to the Greenville Bluesmen, of the Texas-Louisiana League, in exchange for a player to be named later, cash, and ten pounds of catfish. The Suns management showed common sense by not mentioning the fishy aspect of the trade to Krahenbuhl as he prepared for the journey to Mississippi.

"On July 22, I'm traded," Krahenbuhl told *The Sporting News*. "I take four planes. From LA to El Paso to Houston to Jackson, Miss. I drive for two hours to Greenville and I sleep a couple of hours and go to the ball park when they say they're working out the deal so I can pitch that night.

"Now it's two hours before the game and they tell me about the catfish. I'm hot. The Suns could have gotten some player in exchange for me to help their ball club instead of the stinking catfish. Any player that gets traded for a couple fish is not going to like it. It's on my mind the entire game."

As luck might have it, in his debut for Greenville, Catfish Kenny faced the best team in the league, the Amarillo Dillas, and rain delayed the start of the game. But once the contest began, the angry Krahenbuhl pitched the game of his career, not surrendering a hit, or even a base runner. He was perfect.

"I knew I had a no-hitter going," he continued. "We've got a 1-0 lead and by the ninth there's water on the infield. Two out and a guy hits a soft liner at our shortstop who throws the guy out."

"Take that, Oxnard," was the first thing Krahenbuhl said as his perfect game concluded.

Not a bad way to break in with a new team. And when you are traded for ten pounds of catfish and throw a gem in your first outing with the new club, the folks from *Letterman* and *Good Morning America* will come calling.

GOBBLING UP AN OUTFIELDER

A mediocre former major league hurler named Joe Engel became the owner of the Chattanooga Lookouts following his playing career. Known as the Baron of Ballyhoo, Engel once staged a fake safari at his stadium which was highlighted by papier mâché elephants. Another time during the Great Depression, more than 24,000 people jammed into his 10,000-seat stadium as part of a contest to win a house.

But in 1930, he reached a new level. That was when he traded outfielder Johnny "Skins" Jones for a live twenty-five-pound turkey. Jones was certainly no turkey, being talented enough to earn two cups of coffee in the major leagues with the Philadelphia Athletics, where he hit .200 with the club in 1923 and 1932.

TRADED BETWEEN GAMES OF A TWIN BILL

Max Flack was an outfielder who hit .278 in his twelve-year major league career, most of which was spent playing for the Chicago

Cubs. A regular with the team since 1914, Flack and the Cubs were hosting the St. Louis Cardinals in a morning/afternoon doubleheader on Memorial Day of 1922. After going hitless in the first game, Flack went to his home, just three blocks from the stadium, for lunch. Imagine his surprise upon returning to the park to discover that he had been traded to the Cardinals in exchange for outfielder Cliff Heathcote.

The players changed locker rooms and uniforms and played in the second game of the twin bill for their new teams. While neither player had a hit in their final game for their old teams, Flack went 1-for-4 in his Cards debut and Heathcote was 2-for-4 in his Cubs debut.

The deal helped both clubs as the players played better for their new teams. After hitting .222 for Chicago, Flack hit .292 the rest of the way in St. Louis. Heathcote, who was hitting .245 at the time of the deal, hit .280 for the Cubs.

ONE DAY, TWO TEAMS, AND TWO HITS AGAINST HALL OF FAME HURLERS

Unlike Max Flack and Cliff Heathcote, who played for two different teams on the same day and who both failed to get hits in their final game with their former clubs, Joel Youngblood became the first player to get a hit for two different clubs on the same day. Youngblood and his New York Mets teammates were playing an afternoon game at Wrigley Field against the Cubs on August 4, 1982.

During the game in which he hit safely, he was traded to the Montreal Expos in exchange for pitcher Tom Gorman. So Youngblood hopped on a plane and flew to Philadelphia to join the Expos, who were playing a night game against the Phillies. He got there in time to get a pinch hit single to become the first player to get hits for two different clubs on the same day.

Considering the pitchers he got hits against that day, the feat was even more remarkable. In his final game with the Mets, Youngblood got a hit against Ferguson Jenkins. And in his inaugural appearance with the Expos, he hit safely against Steve Carlton. Both pitchers are now members of the Baseball Hall of Fame.

WHEN NEWS OF A TRADE LEAKS OUT

As the son of the former president of the National League, Warren Giles, Bill Giles has lived his entire life in baseball. As a result, he can think on his feet. That truth was evidenced in 1983 when Giles had dual duties acting as CFO of the Philadelphia Phillies as well as the general manager. He and Trader Jack McKeon of the San Diego Padres orchestrated a deal in one of the most unique locales ever.

"When I was playing GM as well as CFO, I once made a trade with Jack McKeon of the Padres when we were both taking a leak at the urinal," said Giles. "We [the Phillies] traded a left-handed relief pitcher named Sid Monge for a pretty good utility player named Joe Lefebvre."

Neither Giles nor McKeon would say whether or not they shook on the deal.

PIMP MY INFIELDER

When the St. Louis Browns had spring training in Montgomery, Alabama, in 1913, the club was undergoing some financial difficulties and was unable to pay the rent at the ballpark. While they were unable to come up with the cash necessary to satisfy their rent bill, there was an alternative. Before the start of the regular season, they traded infielder Clyde "Buzzy" Wares to the Montgomery Black Sox in exchange for the rent. A fine minor league player, Wares had hit .275 for the Black Sox the previous season. He was promoted to St. Louis at the end of the 1913 season, appearing in eleven games and hitting .286.

The following season, Wares spent the entire year in St. Louis, hitting just .209 in eighty-one games. But he showed his heady style of play by pulling the hidden ball trick against Amos Strunk of Philadelphia on May 26.

Wares certainly had the last laugh as he served as a coach in St. Louis after his playing career ended, 1930–1935 and 1937–1951. During his tenure as a coach, he was part of seven St. Louis World Series clubs.

UNSHAKING A HANDSHAKE

During the winter meetings of 1974, an interesting trade was made between the Detroit Tigers and the Philadelphia Phillies. Tigers general manager Jim Campbell and his Phillies counterpart Paul Owens got into a prolonged drinking bout/negotiating session. Owens made no secret of the fact that his best weapon was his ability to out-drink the other general manager. In fact, the Phillies were the champions of that style of trading. At the end of a long session, the two GMs shook hands on a deal that would have sent pitcher Larry Christenson and catcher Bob Boone from the Phillies to Detroit in exchange for veteran catcher Bill Freehan and outfielder Jim Northrup. The Tigers even scheduled a press conference the next day to announce the trade.

"Ruly Carpenter had taken over ownership of the Phillies by then and he went to an old boys' club dinner and had been gone for the entire day," recalled Bill Conlin, of the *Philadelphia Daily News*. "He came back late that night and scout Hugh Alexander breaks the news that two of his favorite players, Christenson and Boone, had been traded. Freehan was clearly on the downhill side and Northrup was a nice complementary outfielder. Well, Ruly went ballistic. He called Jim Campbell and said that his GM was drunk and did not clear the trade with him and the deal is off.

"Campbell was the one who coined a great phrase when he asked, 'I have just one question. How do you unshake a handshake?'"

BEING TRADED FOR SOMEONE VERY IMPORTANT TO YOU

When a player is traded, one of the first questions he asks is, "Who was I traded for?" A few players in the history of the game could not have asked for a better player to be traded for—themselves.

There are countless instances where players are sent to different teams in exchange for a player to be named later. Either the clubs could not agree on which player would be traded, or the team acquiring a new player might want to see how he performs before finalizing their portion of the exchange. When a player is dealt for a player to be named later, the transaction must be completed within six months. Also, the player named can't be playing in the same league he is traded to. So the only way to complete a trade for a player to be named later is by making the deal with a team in the other league.

In April of 1962, the expansion New York Mets of the National League acquired catcher Harry Chiti from the American League's Cleveland Indians for a player to be named later. Chiti was a fine defensive catcher who was adept at receiving the knuckleball. He hit .238 during his ten-year major league career.

After appearing in fifteen games for the Mets, in which he hit .195, the burly catcher was sent back to Cleveland on June 15 as the player to be named in the trade for Chiti. It was the first time a player was traded for himself.

Dickie Noles had a 36-53 record during his eleven-year career with Philadelphia, the Chicago Cubs, Texas, Cleveland, Detroit, and Baltimore. He may be best known for being credited with turning the momentum of the 1980 World Series in favor of the Phillies when he brushed back hot-hitting George Brett in game four of that Fall Classic which saw Philadelphia win its only World Series title.

With a 4-2 record in forty-one games while pitching for the Chicago Cubs in 1987, Noles was dealt to the Detroit Tigers on September 22 for a player to be named later. A month and a day after heading to Detroit, Noles was sent back to the Cubs as the player to be named after appearing in just four games for the Tigers.

Since his career ended, Noles has become a motivational speaker and the Phillies' employee assistance professional. A recovering alcoholic who has said that his disease prematurely ended his career, Noles helps players who are battling addictions or experiencing mental or emotional stress.

During his major league career, Dickie Noles had eleven saves. It seems certain that since throwing his last pitch in the major leagues in 1990, he has far exceeded those eleven saves he earned on the mound.

A BROADCASTING DEAL

Weird trades have not been limited to player for player, player for outfield fence, or player for live turkey. Some deals have gone in different directions altogether. Consider, for instance, the deal that saw long-time Detroit Tigers announcer Ernie Harwell traded to the major leagues in exchange for a player.

When Harwell was a young man announcing games for the Double A Atlanta Crackers of the Southern Association in 1948, Brooklyn Dodgers announcer Red Barber became ill. Branch Rickey contacted Atlanta owner Earl Mann to see if he would allow Harwell to join the major league Brooklyn team. Mann agreed, but only if the Dodgers sent minor league catcher Cliff

Dapper, who had been toiling in Montreal, to Atlanta in exchange for Harwell. Rickey agreed and the deal was done.

Harwell started what would be a fifty-five-year major league broadcasting career on August 4, 1948, when he called the Dodgers-Cubs game. A long-time minor league player, Cliff Dapper had seen big-league action only for a short time in 1942. He made the most of his chance, getting eight hits in seventeen at bats for Brooklyn, which translated into a lofty .471 career big-league batting average.

At Harwell's retirement celebration in Detroit in 2002, the Tigers brought in Dapper, who was eighty-two at the time, to finally meet Ernie Harwell.

AT LEAST HE CAN DESCRIBE WHY WE CAN'T WIN

Another strange transaction was orchestrated by Chicago Cubs owner Phil Wrigley that saw him trade his manager in exchange for a radio announcer. With the Cubs struggling with a 6-11 record in May of 1960, Wrigley sent manager Charlie Grimm to the Cubs' broadcasting booth to replace Hall of Fame player Lou Boudreau, who succeeded Grimm as the Cubs' skipper.

Grimm remained with the Cubs organization for fifteen more years in various front-office positions. Boudreau managed the team to a 54-83 record for the remainder of the season. Upon his death in 1983, the Cubs agreed to allow the widow of Charlie Grimm to scatter his ashes over his beloved Wrigley Field.

THE BACKSTOP FOR THE SKIPPER

Another strange situation occurred on November 5, 1976, when Oakland A's manager Chuck Tanner was, in essence, traded to the Pittsburgh Pirates in exchange for catcher Manny Sanguillen.

Tanner was a veteran big-league skipper who had piloted the Chicago White Sox from 1970 to 1975 with a 401-414 record. He took the reins of the A's in 1976 and guided them to a second-place finish and an impressive 87-74 record. That's when the Pirates came calling and Tanner was allowed to go to the Steel City along with $100,000 in exchange for Sanguillen, a fine catcher and clutch hitter who had spent the previous nine seasons with the Pirates.

From 1977 to 1985, Chuck Tanner amassed a 711-685 record with Pittsburgh, including a world championship. He remains one of the most popular and respected members of the Pirates.

Ironically, following the 1977 season in which Sanguillen hit .275 in 152 games for Oakland, he was traded back to the Pirates in April 1978 in exchange for Miguel Dilone, Elias Sosa, and a player to be named later, Mike Edwards.

TAKE MY WIFE . . . PLEASE

Perhaps the strangest trade in the history of Major League Baseball was not made by owners or general managers. This deal, which was consummated in 1973, was made by two New York Yankees pitchers, Fritz Peterson and Mike Kekich. The two hurlers traded their families and homes. Kekich acquired Marilyn Peterson, her two children, and their family poodle in exchange for Susanne Kekich, her two children, and their family Bedlington terrier.

The players had become good friends while members of the Yankees' pitching staff, often double-dating with their spouses. Jokes about wife-swapping soon turned into reality and the players announced their life-swap in spring training of 1973. Peterson pitched for eleven seasons with a 133-131 record accumulated for the Yankees, Cleveland, and Texas. Kekich had a nine-year career with a mediocre 39-51 record with the Yankees, Dodgers, Indians, Rangers, and Mariners.

Mike Kekich and Marilyn Peterson soon broke up. He is now remarried and living in New Mexico where he has worked as an insurance adjuster. Fritz Peterson and Susanne Kekich were married in 1974 and have four children of their own. He has worked on a casino boat in Elgin, Illinois.

After the trade was made public, Yankees general manager Lee McPhail, who must have felt left out by the process, quipped, "We may have to call off Family Day."

It should be noted that in the proudest and truest tradition of the game of baseball, both Peterson and Kekich were southpaws.

❚❚

THE FINAL SCORE

Is the Game Better?

The battle for power in Major League Baseball has been an epic struggle that has seen the pendulum of power swing from favoring the players to the owners and now back to the players again. That a constant battle such as this could go on for so many years while the game of baseball continues to be America's Game is a testament to the game itself and its fans. For regardless of whether it was the owners who had the ultimate control over the game, or the players, after they became millionaire vagabonds, with even the most pedestrian of players earning tens of millions of dollars, the fans have remained.

That loyalty is a labor of love because while the game remains the same, it is also very different. In earlier years players were just like the fans, earning a good living but still needing to have employment of some sort in the off-season. They were the same as us and easy to relate to and root for. But thanks to their powerful union and the advances made by Marvin Miller, today's players have become rich recluses who have little in common with the common fan. Many earn more in a day than most of us earn in a year, making it much more difficult to relate to the player of today. Plus players change teams like most of the rest of us change radio stations.

The game itself still largely resembles the game that the New York Knickerbockers played during the 1840s. While much has changed, it's still the same basic, beautiful game at heart. The pitching box is raised and farther away and base runners aren't plugged anymore. But four balls still equal a walk and three strikes mean an out, especially since Ted Williams didn't jump to the Mexican League. The two- or three-inning save is gone forever and the specialization of baseball continues to make many of the players something less than complete players. But it's still baseball.

In years gone by, it was possible to bring the family out to enjoy a baseball game and come away from the experience feeling as though you got your money's worth. Those days are gone forever as the ultimate cost of the mega-million-dollar contracts and the tens of millions of dollar team budgets have trickled down to the turnstiles and the fans. Not all that long ago, a family of four could enjoy a game from soup to nuts for less than $100. Now, to get premium seating and park the car, we're starting out at somewhere between $180 and $200 at most big-league stadiums.

Try finding a soda for less than $6, and a beer and a dog will bite you for anywhere between $12 and $15. A family night at the ballpark is not an inexpensive way to enjoy some good family time. But the game remains the real draw, even though stadiums now have luxury suite after luxury suite for the big spenders. Thankfully, no matter how many millions of dollars your second baseman might be making, on most nights he'll still hang in there to complete a double play and bust it trying to advance from first to third on a single to right field.

Perhaps that is the reason for the continued popularity of baseball. In 2006, more baseball fans passed through the turnstiles at ballparks than ever before. For the third consecutive season, a new single-season attendance record was set as 76,043,902 fans attended big-league games. That represented a 1.5 percent increase over the previous season, when 74,926,174 people attended a game. In addition, consider that the average ticket price to attend a game is $22. So gate receipts alone came in at $1.9 billion in 2006, an 8 percent increase over the previous year.

Seven teams drew more than 3 million fans in 2006 and fourteen teams drew at least 2.5 million fans, while twenty-five of the thirty major league teams drew more than 2 million. Every major league team drew at least 1 million fans. The New York Yankees saw more than 4 million fans attend games at the House That Ruth Built. Boston became the first major league team to set a home attendance record for seven consecutive seasons. The New York Mets drew more than 3.4 million, giving New York a total of more than 7.5 million fans in 162 dates. It's not just the Mets that were Amazin'.

Out on the West Coast, the Los Angeles Dodgers played in front of a franchise record 3,758,431 fans and the Los Angeles Angels of Anaheim drew 3,318,745. Chicago was no slouch either, as the White Sox drew 2,957,414 fans while the Cubs drew in excess of 3 million fans for the third consecutive season.

Four years ago, Major League Baseball teams lost about $57 million. But steroid scandals and mega-million-dollar deals for players notwithstanding, the game is back and better than ever. In 2006, baseball enjoyed record earnings of $496 million. That's quite a turnaround. It's no small wonder that Bud Selig has hung around for so long.

Cable television fees represent a huge payday for major league clubs. Fox's regional cable sports network has the rights to televise games of nineteen teams and paid $257 million in fees. The Yankees made $67 million from the YES network, while their crosstown rivals, the Mets, brought in $47 million during the inaugural year of SportsNet New York. Up in Boston, the Red Sox got $21 million in rights fees, while the Chicago Cubs made $20 million from WGN and an additional $20 million from Comcast.

While baseball is a $6 billion business, it remains the kindest and simplest of sports, offering a familiarity and comfort level of no other. Through all of the changes and issues with the control of power, the game continues. And while arbitration and free agency have forever changed the face of the game, players come and go and, as has always been the case, teams need to make trades. But the act of making player transactions is now forever tied to the freedoms that the players wrestled away from ownership in the 1970s. In baseball's brave new world, many trades are dictated by the contract status of the players involved. In the final analysis, is baseball better now than it was when the owners were czars of the game?

"In all honesty, Jim Gott the fan fears that the game may have hurt itself by pricing itself out of having every kid who loves baseball and every family member who loves the game and every significant other who enjoys the game from being able to just sit at the ballpark and experience the common bond that baseball provides," Gott said. "One of the great experiences is to be able to sit there and watch the game and talk about the players. The game has changed so much, not only financially, but not having the same composition of teams. When I was younger you knew the Dodgers infield would always have Cey, Russell, Lopes, and Garvey.

"Now things are much more accelerated because of the financial situation. General managers have so much pressure to perform. The owners want their players to perform and rightly so. But it's different. In the old days you'd have the same infield for seven or eight straight years. It's not that way anymore and the fans miss that.

"From the perspective of a former player, I was able to play fourteen years in the big leagues, where had I played a generation before, I might have played only four or five years because of my performance. You'd have to get a lot of wins in the minor leagues and then hope to get a veteran player's spot in the majors. So many of my opportunities to have baseball as a career, not to mention the many positive aspects of my life, are due to the changes that occurred to the game. Owners and general managers are now forced to make decisions about letting people become free agents, in both the minor and major leagues, that they never had to make before. Now you can have a team risk $50,000 to give a player like me a shot at spring training as a Rule 5 draft choice. It allowed me to be in the position I'm in now. I had two major injuries in my career that kept me out for a full season. But thanks to Curt Flood, the team could not just give up on me and I had the chance to come back and perform, which I was able to do."

Has free agency, the single most powerful labor/ownership struggle of the twentieth century, been as good for the game as it has been for the players? Like anything else, it depends on whom you talk to.

"You could actually make a good argument both ways," said Bill Giles. "It gives you as an organization an opportunity to quickly improve your team if you want to spend the money. I think that free agency does provide a system where a team can improve itself dramatically even if they don't have any players in their farm system. You have to say that's a positive thing. In the old days, if you didn't have a good farm system, you'd be in trouble for years. Now, a team with no talent in the farm system can get better by signing free agents.

"The negative is that a lot of people complain that players jump around and you can't keep track of your favorite players, which is exaggerated. You have to have a balance. Free agency has changed the economy of the game, which has gone crazy. When players get too much money, like Alfonso Soriano, who is getting $134 million, there is pressure put on by your attendance. If the attendance goes down, your team goes down.

"One of the reasons the power of the players has gone up is the need to build new ballparks. You see teams overpay players to improve the perception of the team, which helps get new ballparks built. Concessions and premium seats are a big part of your profit and loss statement. New ballparks with premium seats generate lots of money."

To be sure, much of the money that has been generated is now shared by ownership and the players. Judging by attendance, television ratings, and the basic health of the business, it can be argued that the game continues to prosper. But the little guy continues to foot the bill. Players move around from season to season no longer developing long-term relationships with the fans of their cities. That is one of the trappings of free agency. So is the game really better because of it?

"As a fan, I have to say no," said Jerrold Casway. "I grew up a Phillies fan and in those days the players stayed with the same team for their whole careers. That's how you related to your team. They grew their own talent. Now it's totally out of hand. A guy like Jim Thome can come in and get $80 million. Now he's gone. What would Koufax or Mays get in today's game? It boggles the mind. In many respects, this has hurt the game."

Some of those same sentiments were echoed by respected veteran general manager Pat Gillick. But while he agrees with some concerns of the fans, he also has a feel for some of the positive effects that change has had on the game.

"For those who were fans of the game thirty years ago, the game is probably not better than it was," he said. "Fans like to see a Mike Schmidt, or a Kenny Boyer, or a Ted Williams play with the same team for a long period of time. With free agency, there is a great deal more movement and those players who stay in the same city are few and far between, such as the Cal Ripkins and the Tony Gwynns.

"But overall, I think you'd have to say that it's been good for baseball and I think that baseball has prospered. So I think that it's something that some of the old-timers like myself have to become more accustomed to."

Even though he cashed in as an early free agent toward the end of his career, pitcher Rick Wise is a lifelong fan of the game who has concerns about where the game is headed.

"No, it's not better," Wise said. "It's better for the players. Guys have no-trade clauses and are making so much money. It's so different now from when I played that I don't even worry about it. We didn't have agents and players stayed with the same organization. We had no freedom of movement.

"It's hard to compare eras. I will say that I would never trade the era I played for anything. There were a lot of great players who didn't make a lot of money. Some of the greatest players that ever played the game played in my era. I remember when I was breaking in there were players like Ernie Banks, Willie Mays, Willie McCovey, Eddie Matthews, Hank Aaron, and Billy Williams. It seemed like every team had at least one Hall of Fame–caliber player, or at least near–Hall of Famers. They were outstanding ballplayers and great fellows who loved the game of baseball the way I have since I was five years old. I was fortunate to come along at that point.

"Things have changed in the workplace all over the world and baseball is no exception. That is the reality. All I concentrate on now as a pitching coach is what's on the field. When I put the uniform on to work with my pitchers, I find that is the game at its purest. My passion for the game is still what it always was. That's why I'm still riding buses as a minor league pitching coach after all these years."

Before passing judgment on the game of baseball in the new millennium, it's important to think about how teams try to build championship-caliber clubs. In this obscene new world of baseball, money talks and everything else walks. But just because a team has money, there is more to building a championship club than having eight overpaid and sometimes underachieving All-Stars on the field. No matter how much a team's payroll might be, there is still no guarantee the whole will come anywhere near to equaling the sum of its parts.

Sometimes the single element that gives one team the ultimate advantage over another in the standings is something that does not show up in the box score. For every time a Barry Bonds has driven home a key run or smacked a tape-measure tater, there is a Dick Groat who selflessly gives himself up and hits the ball on the right side of the infield to advance a runner into scoring position. The hit or the homer can get you a run. Advancing the runner can lead to a big inning by keeping your team out of a double-play situation.

A long-standing truth in life also holds true in baseball. There is an ingredient that is arguably much more important than talent. And that ingredient is chemistry.

"I've seen too many teams, the classic example is the current Chicago Cubs squad, try to build an All-Star team and assume if you have the best players, you'll walk to a pennant," said Bill Conlin. "Guys that know and trust each other and allow a leader to step forward and run the clubhouse are more important. I much prefer the approach where if you had a good team, like the Yankees always did back in the day, that led to tremendous continuity. The sense that Ruth was going to be in the three hole and that Gehrig was going to be in the four hole and that Lazzeri was in the six hole. You'd have a great catcher and four dependable starters who could be counted on to give you nine innings or pretty damn close. I much prefer that approach to baseball.

"On the other hand, it's nice to be a club that has a pressing need and the money to fill that need. Suppose we need a great third baseman and Scott Rolen appears unhappy in Philadelphia. Let me negotiate to get him. It's nice to have the money and the flexibility to go out and get a Curt Schilling, as the Diamondbacks did. Or, to be a George Steinbrenner, where money is no object. You can fill needs with your wallet, rather than your farm system. But at the same exact time, you put money into the farm system.

"The perfect way to go into this era is to have the money to sign who you need and fill out the rest of your roster with your minor league investment. I grew up with the boys of summer and I much prefer players like Pee Wee Reese and Carl Furillo, who you knew were always going to be there. I'm a purist in that way but do acknowledge that money does have the power to win pennants and does so in this era."

Eras change and the business of baseball changes. Building a championship ball club, or at least a team that can compete, has become a very different exercise for baseball executives. The days of trading players to improve your team or rid the squad of a troublemaker are few and far between. In this day and age of baseball, it seems that the majority of trades are made because players are coming up to the end of their existing contracts, which in many cases means impending free agency.

Arbitration hassles have drastically increased salaries in Major League Baseball. But it is the six-year window that clubs can hold onto a player that has become perhaps the driving force behind most trades.

"Arbitration and free agency have been great for the players, but not necessarily for the game," said Larry Colton. "There is no loyalty today. Players are more like invading armies. They come into their towns and take whatever they can. Then they pack up and move on. They are rarely community citizens.

"It's true that the players are bigger, faster, and stronger today. I'm glad I don't have to pitch against them, especially with the 46 mph fastball I'm now featuring. For the most part, they take better care of themselves than players of my era did. The stakes are so much higher now. If a player can last just a couple of years in the bigs, he has a chance to be set for life.

"Money was almost no factor when I played. It's a tired cliché, but I was just happy to be getting paid for playing a game I loved so much. Sure, I wanted to get paid more, but my theory was that all I had to do was be really good and I'd get paid really well. If I was playing today, I doubt I would have quit, which I did in part because I was tired of trying to make the leap past Triple A to get back to the Show and because I felt I needed to do something more socially relevant with my life. If the minimum big-league salary back then would have been something like $400,000 as it is today [it was $10,000 back then], I probably would have somehow rationalized that a career in the bigs was all the social relevance I needed."

Is the game better? Purists will argue in the negative because of the lack of fundamentals exhibited at the major league level and because it is increasingly difficult to recognize a quarter of every roster from year to year. But the facts seem to indicate that people are flocking to the ballpark in record numbers. The Wild Card races have added intrigue and suspense to the season, keeping races in question until the season's final weekend.

Teams are making money, players are making money, and fans don't seem to mind spending money to watch games in person or on television as part of an extended cable TV package. At the end of the day, it really doesn't matter if the game is better or not. All that matters is that fans are interested and that the game is popular.

Say what you will about football, basketball, hockey, and college athletics. There is simply nothing that even comes close to Major League Baseball.

12

PLAYERS SOON TO
BE ON THE MOVE?

The walls of casinos in Las Vegas, Atlantic City, and other gambling venues are filled with people who like to try their luck at the various gaming tables. Many feel that they have a system that will enable them to overcome the odds and walk away a big winner. Most walk away with a feeling of what could have been, or what wasn't even close to being. After all, the lights that brighten up these gambling meccas were not paid for by the players who won.

The same casinos are also havens for sports fans to get their fix in the various sports books which offer a constant collection of various sporting events, games, and races to give even the most serious sports addict a full plate of material to enjoy. And like the gamblers who are sure that their system will result in winnings beyond belief, the die-hard sports fan also has been known to put his or her reputation on the line with legal betting on their favorite sport.

While the odds-makers ensure that winning at sports betting is kept to a minimum, we all know beyond the shadow of a doubt which teams will be part of baseball's postseason extravaganza. Fifty dollars here and fifty dollars there will result in a nice payday from the casino after the World Series is completed, somewhere around Thanksgiving. Of course, injuries, slumps, and countless other factors enter into the way the postseason ultimately finishes. Turns out we didn't know after all. That's why they play the game.

While it is always a crapshoot as to which teams will finish in playoff contention, as the evolution of the game of baseball continues, it becomes easier to predict which players will be most likely to leave their current ball clubs. As has been discussed earlier, the prospect of losing a free-agent-to-be whom you know your organization cannot extend beyond his expiring contract leads to trading players to other clubs who might have a chance to sign the player, or who are willing to rent him for a few months in search of that postseason dream.

This past off-season, a number of impact players had their contracts expire with the clubs they started the 2007 season playing with. Consider some of these names. Did they finish out the season, or were they traded in an effort by their club to get some value in return?

Players eligible for free agency following the 2007 season included the likes of Carlos Zambrano, Joe Nathan, Mariano Rivera, Jorge Posada, Curt Schilling, Bobby Abreu, Ichiro Suzuki, Andrew Jones, and Carlos Guillen. That's quite a collection of very talented players, all of which were strong candidates to be re-signed by the same club they started the season with.

But consider another list of players who were available for the free agent market following the 2007 campaign. This list includes Jason Jennings, Ivan Rodriguez, Freddy Garcia, Torii Hunter, Jason Isringhausen, Paul Lo Duca, Adam Dunn, Scott Linebrink, Jon Lieber, and Aaron Rowand. A quick roster check might show that some of these players have been on the move.

Instead of considering which teams will qualify for the playoffs via division championships and Wild Card races in 2008, why not take a look at a list of some of the players who will be eligible for free agency at the end of the season? Certainly, a large number of these players will ultimately remain with their current teams. But a study of this collection of players will give a good base to look at when considering who has the best chance of being moved before the end of the season. Much like the previous lists, it's difficult, if not impossible, to imagine some of these players with different organizations. But this is the new era of baseball, where what used to be is no more.

Consider some of these players as guys who could be on the move. There is Ken Griffey Jr., Vladimir Guerrero, Travis Hafner, Chipper Jones, Pedro Martinez, Orlando Cabrera, Jon Garland, Joe Crede, Carlos Delgado, Nomar Garciaparra, Johnny Estrada, Troy Glaus, Jason Varitek, Jim Thome, Mark Mulder, Jake Peavy, Ben Sheets, Manny Ramirez, Johan Santana, Edgar Renteria, and Francisco Rodriguez. That could also be a list of multiple future Hall of Famers.

There are numerous other players who will be eligible for free agency following the 2008 season. This impressive group includes, Garret Anderson, Rich Aurilia, Rocco Baldelli, Hank Blalock, Pat Burrell, Endy Chavez, Alex Cintron, Alex Cora, Craig Counsell, Carl Crawford, Ryan Dempster, Brendan Donnelly, Ray Durham, Juan Encarnacion, Adam Everett, Kyle Farnsworth, Brian Fuentes, Bob Howry, Brad Lidge, Derek Lowe, Mike Maroth, Kevin Mench, Jason Michaels, Wily Mo Pena, Oliver Perez, A. J. Pierzynski, Scott Podsednik, Nick Punta, and Salomon Torres.

Any team in baseball could improve its roster by making additions from these groups of players. All it will cost is money and there will be more than one bidder for their services. Some of the players will take advantage of "contract" years and guarantee themselves a payday of immense proportions. Some of the more pedestrian role players will also get outstanding deals to do what they do best. A good team could get over the hump by making the right decisions regarding these players and a bad team could become a contender overnight. That is if they spend wisely and build a team based not only on talent, but also on chemistry.

So keep a scorecard for some of the players listed above and see if baseball's brave new world has them on the move.

SOURCES

Allen, Dick. *Crash: The Life and Times of Dick Allen*. New York: Ticknor & Fields, 1989.

Casway, Jerrold. *Ed Delahanty in the Emerald Age of Baseball*. Notre Dame, Ind.: University of Notre Dame Press, 2004.

Claire, Fred. *My 30 Years in Dodger Blue*. Champaign, Ill.: Sports Publishing, 2004.

Devine, Bing. *The Memoirs of Bing Devine*. Champaign, Ill.: Sports Publishing, 2004.

Eckler, John. "Baseball—Sport or Commerce?" In *The Second Fireside Book of Baseball*. New York: Simon and Schuster, 1958.

Gilbert, Bill. "Salary Arbitration: Burden or Benefit?" In *Nickel & Dime Pitches*. Cleveland, Ohio: University of Nebraska Press, 2007.

Giles, Bill. *Pouring Six Beers at a Time and Other Stories from a Lifetime in Baseball*. Chicago, Ill.: Triumph Books, 2007.

Gordon, Spencer B. "Final Offer Arbitration in the New Era of Major League Baseball." Pepperdine School of Law, 2006.

Mandell, David. "Danny Gardella and the Reserve Clause." In *The National Pastime: A Review of Baseball History*. Kent, Ohio: Society for Baseball Research, 2006.

McCarver, Tim. *Baseball for Brain Surgeons and Other Fans*. New York: Villard, 1998.

Pluto, Terry. *The Curse of Rocky Colavito*. New York: Simon & Schuster, 1994.

———. *Our Tribe*. New York: Simon & Schuster, 1999.

Rains, Rob. *The St. Louis Cardinals: The 100th Anniversary History.* New York: St. Martin's Press, 1992.

Schmidt, Mike. *Clearing the Bases.* New York: HarperCollins, 2006.

Schuerholz, John. *Built to Win.* New York: Warner Books, 2006.

Thornley, Stew. "The Demise of the Reserve Clause." In *Nickel & Dime Pitches*. Cleveland, Ohio: University of Nebraska Press, 2007.

Vecsey, George. *Baseball: A History of America's Favorite Game.* New York: Random House, 2006.

Zimniuch, Fran. *Phillies, Where Have You Gone?* Champaign, Ill.: Sports Publishing, 2004.

INDEX